Praise for *TIBCO® Architecture Fundamentals*

W9-BMZ-576

"*TIBCO® Architecture Fundamentals* is a must-read for anybody involved with the architecture and design of distributed systems, with system integration issues, or with service-based application design. In particular, solution architects responsible for TIBCO-based systems architectures should consider reading this book and its planned follow-on titles.

"The product portfolio of TIBCO today is simply too broad for anybody to have an ongoing detailed understanding of what is in there and what elements of the portfolio are best suited in a given business scenario. Paul Brown provides the required oversight in this book, helping both experienced solution architects and newcomers in the field find their way through the myriad technology options TIBCO offers today."

—*Bert Hooyman, Chief Architect, Europe for MphasiS (an HP Company)*

"In his previous books, Dr. Brown developed the 'total architecture concept' in a generic setting. In this one, he presents a concrete application of it to the TIBCO product line. It will be a valuable resource to anyone developing solutions with those tools."

—*Glenn Smith, Principal Consultant, Appian*

"This material is spot on for what is needed in enterprises today, to give a level set to all the architecture teams and project teams they interact with, to outline what is expected, and the roles that each play. In addition, it is a timely overview of the latest TIBCO product suites, and I am anxious to see the follow-ups to this (BusinessEvents- and BPM-focused materials).

"This book provides a detailed look at what happens in the creation of an integration architecture for a business problem. Paul's attempt to capture in words the years of project experience will be a benefit for groups getting familiar with establishing an enterprise architecture standard, as well as a refresher for those performing this function today.

"I would like for all the folks on my team to read this to ensure we are all on the same page with the deliverables that are expected from architecture teams involved in global projects, and the role that the TIBCO tools play in implementing these solutions."

—*Joseph G. Meyer, Director of Architecture Services and R&D, Citi*

"Brown's approach to presenting the highly complex architectural issues is by far the best I have encountered. While each of the individual areas has been detailed in other texts, this is the only publication I have read that lays out each aspect of the architectural issues and describes them in an easy-to-read, comfortable style."

—*James G. Keegan Jr., President, Intrepico, Inc.*

"I recommend the book wholeheartedly. The combination of breadth and depth is not usually found in technical books."

—*Lloyd Fischer, Senior Software Architect, WellCare Health Plans*

TIBCO® Architecture Fundamentals

To Pong,
Help customers build total
architectures with TIBCO!

— Paul

TIBCO® Architecture Fundamentals

Paul C. Brown

✦✦ Addison-Wesley

Upper Saddle River, NJ • Boston • Indianapolis • San Francisco
New York • Toronto • Montreal • London • Munich • Paris • Madrid
Capetown • Sydney • Tokyo • Singapore • Mexico City

TIB, TIBCO, TIBCO Software, TIBCO Adapter, Predictive Business, Information Bus, The Power of Now, TIBCO ActiveMatrix® Adapter for Database, TIBCO ActiveMatrix® Adapter for Files (Unix/Win), TIBCO ActiveMatrix® Adapter for IBM I, TIBCO ActiveMatrix® Adapter for Kenan BP, TIBCO ActiveMatrix® Adapter for Lotus Notes, TIBCO ActiveMatrix® Adapter for PeopleSoft, TIBCO ActiveMatrix® Adapter for SAP, TIBCO ActiveMatrix® Adapter for Tuxedo, TIBCO ActiveMatrix® Adapter for WebSphere MQ, TIBCO ActiveMatrix® Administrator, TIBCO ActiveMatrix® Binding Type for Adapter, TIBCO ActiveMatrix® Binding Type for EJB, TIBCO ActiveMatrix® BPM, TIBCO ActiveMatrix BusinessWorks™, TIBCO ActiveMatrix BusinessWorks™ BPEL Extension, TIBCO ActiveMatrix BusinessWorks™ Service Engine, TIBCO ActiveMatrix® Implementation Type for C++, TIBCO ActiveMatrix® Lifecycle Governance Framework, TIBCO ActiveMatrix® Service Bus, TIBCO ActiveMatrix® Service Grid, TIBCO® Adapter for CICS, TIBCO® Adapter for Clarify, TIBCO® Adapter for COM, TIBCO® Adapter for CORBA, TIBCO® Adapter for EJB, TIBCO® Adapter for Files i5/OS, TIBCO® Adapter for Files z/OS (MVS), TIBCO® Adapter for Infranet, TIBCO® Adapter for JDE OneWorld Xe, TIBCO® Adapter for Remedy, TIBCO® Adapter SDK, TIBCO® Adapter for Siebel, TIBCO® Adapter for SWIFT, TIBCO® Adapter for Teradata, TIBCO Business Studio™, TIBCO BusinessConnect™, TIBCO BusinessEvents™, TIBCO BusinessEvents™ Data Modeling, TIBCO BusinessEvents™ Decision Manager, TIBCO BusinessEvents™ Event Stream Processing, TIBCO BusinessEvents™ Standard Edition, TIBCO BusinessEvents™ Views, TIBCO BusinessWorks™, TIBCO BusinessWorks™ BPEL Extension, TIBCO BusinessWorks™ SmartMapper, TIBCO BusinessWorks™ XA Transaction Manager, TIBCO Collaborative Information Manager™, TIBCO Enterprise Message Service™, TIBCO Enterprise Message Service™ Central Administration, TIBCO Enterprise Message Service™ OpenVMS Client, TIBCO Enterprise Message Service™ OpenVMS C Client, TIBCO® EMS Client for AS/400, TIBCO® EMS Client for i5/OS, TIBCO® EMS Client for IBM I, TIBCO® EMS Client for z/OS, TIBCO® EMS Client for z/OS (CICS), TIBCO® EMS Client for z/OS (MVS), TIBCO® EMS Transport Channel for WCF, TIBCO® General Interface, TIBCO Rendezvous®, and TIBCO Runtime Agent are either registered trademarks or trademarks of TIBCO Software Inc. and/or its affiliates in the United States and/or other countries.

The author and publisher have taken care in the preparation of this book, but make no expressed or implied warranty of any kind and assume no responsibility for errors or omissions. No liability is assumed for incidental or consequential damages in connection with or arising out of the use of the information or programs contained herein.

The publisher offers excellent discounts on this book when ordered in quantity for bulk purchases or special sales, which may include electronic versions and/or custom covers and content particular to your business, training goals, marketing focus, and branding interests. For more information, please contact:

U.S. Corporate and Government Sales
(800) 382-3419
corpsales@pearsontechgroup.com

For sales outside the United States please contact:

International Sales
international@pearson.com

Visit us on the Web: informit.com/aw

Library of Congress Cataloging-in-Publication Data

Brown, Paul C.
    TIBCO architecture fundamentals / Paul C. Brown.
        p.   cm.
    Includes bibliographical references and index.
    ISBN 978-0-321-77261-9 (pbk. : alk. paper) 1. Service-oriented architecture (Computer science) 2. Business—Data processing. I. Title.
    TK5105.5828.B76 2011
    00.5—dc22

                                                                            2011006244

ISBN-13: 978-0-321-77261-9
ISBN-10:   0-321-77261-X
Text printed in the United States on recycled paper at RR Donnelley in Crawfordsville, Indiana.
First printing, May 2011

For Jessica and Philip,
my most prized creations.

Contents

Preface

About This Book

The subject matter for this book lies at the intersection of three very broad topics: architecture, solutions, and TIBCO products (Figure P-1). Each of these topics, individually, has been the subject of many volumes. The purpose of this book is to begin to tie these three topics together in a very pragmatic way, providing a foundation for architecting solutions with TIBCO products.

This book is not intended to provide a comprehensive introduction into any one of the three broader topic areas. Nevertheless, some coverage of these topics is a necessary prerequisite to discussing the specifics of architecting solutions with TIBCO products. Part I provides an introduction to some of the essential concepts of architecture. Part II provides a cursory overview of the TIBCO product stack and explores the architecture of some of the most broadly used products,

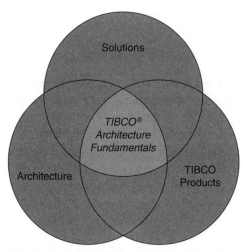

Figure P-1: *Subject Matter for* TIBCO® Architecture Fundamentals

emphasizing information not readily found in the individual product manuals. Part III takes a bottom-up approach to exploring the most basic and commonly found design patterns used in architecting solutions with TIBCO products. Part IV begins the discussion of services and solutions, emphasizing the application of the design patterns discussed earlier.

Solutions built with TIBCO products tend to be distributed solutions involving multiple systems, multiple data stores, and multiple business processes along with the people participating in those business processes. Thus, the discussion in this book covers the structure and organization of both the participants and the work being performed, with particular emphasis on the mapping of the work onto the participants.

TIBCO® Architecture Fundamentals lays the groundwork for architecting these systems. Part I provides simple working definitions for architecture and reference architecture. It discusses the roles to be played by project and enterprise architects, and the measurable reduction in project duration (up to 25%) that can be achieved by paying appropriate attention to architecture. Part II discusses the organization of the major TIBCO products and describes how solutions progress from design into production. Part III uses design patterns to explore dozens of design choices defining how people and systems can interact and coordinate their work. Part IV examines solution architecture, exploring the notion of services and discussing how reference architectures can be applied when building solutions.

TIBCO Architecture Book Series

As the first book in a series, *TIBCO® Architecture Fundamentals* only begins the discussion of architecting solutions with TIBCO products (Figure P-2). It lays the foundation for architecting TIBCO-based solutions and serves as a common foundation for the series. Each of the more advanced books explores a different style of solution, all based on TIBCO technology. Each explores the additional TIBCO products relevant to that style of solution. Each defines larger and more specialized architecture patterns relevant to the style, all built on top of the foundational set of design patterns presented in this book.

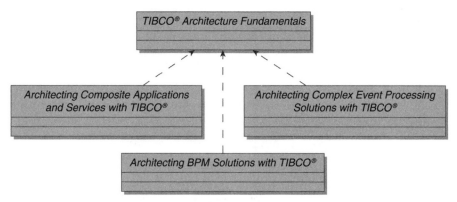

Figure P-2: *Initial TIBCO Architecture Book Series*

Intended Audience

TIBCO® Architecture Fundamentals is written for architects and lead engineers designing solutions in which TIBCO products play a significant role. Enterprise architects will also gain some insight as to how they can employ reference architectures to document design patterns. Such reference architectures give voice to their design intent and serve to efficiently give direction to project teams.

To derive maximum benefit from this book, it is useful for the reader to already have some familiarity with the TIBCO product set. The provided overview of the major TIBCO products and their organization is supplementary and is intended to augment the information contained in the product manuals.

Throughout this book the majority of the diagrams employ UML notations, particularly Class, Activity, and Composite Structure diagrams, with occasional use of other UML notations. For the most part, the meaning of these diagrams should be intuitively obvious, and thus a formal understanding of the UML notation is not a requirement for reading this book. On the other hand, the UML notations have a formality and precision that, when properly understood, allow the reader to extract even more information from the diagrams. The *Unified Modeling Language Reference Manual, Second Edition,*[1] is an excellent reference in this regard.

---

1. James Rumbaugh, Ivar Jacobson, and Grady Booch, *The Unified Modeling Language Reference Manual, Second Edition*, Boston: Addison-Wesley (2004).

Detailed Learning Objectives

After reading this book, you should be able to:

- Explain the design perspective required for modern IT projects and the concepts of total architecture, architecture, and reference architecture

- Predict the positive impact that architecture can have upon project duration, and explain the roles of project and enterprise architects in achieving this benefit

- Explain the basic SCA concepts and read an SCA diagram

- Describe the core TIBCO products: TIBCO Enterprise Message Service™, TIBCO ActiveMatrix® Service Bus, TIBCO ActiveMatrix® Service Grid, TIBCO ActiveMatrix® BPM, and TIBCO BusinessEvents™

- Select appropriate design patterns for basic system interactions and identify and select the appropriate TIBCO products to be used

- Outline the capabilities of policies in TIBCO ActiveMatrix Service Bus

- Select appropriate design patterns for mediation, external system interaction, and coordination of activities

- Explain the concept of a service and the criteria for deciding when an investment in a service is warranted

- Explain how a solution architecture should be characterized and how reference architectures can be applied to the building of solutions

Organization of the Book

The book is structured into four parts, as shown in Figure P-3. Part I covers foundational concepts: architecture, reference architecture, solution architecture, the role of architects, and Service-Component Architecture (SCA). The discussions in this portion of the book are relatively abstract (high level) and technology independent.

Part II covers the architecture of the most commonly used TIBCO products: TIBCO Enterprise Message Service (EMS), the TIBCO Active-Matrix product suite, and TIBCO BusinessEvents. The discussions in

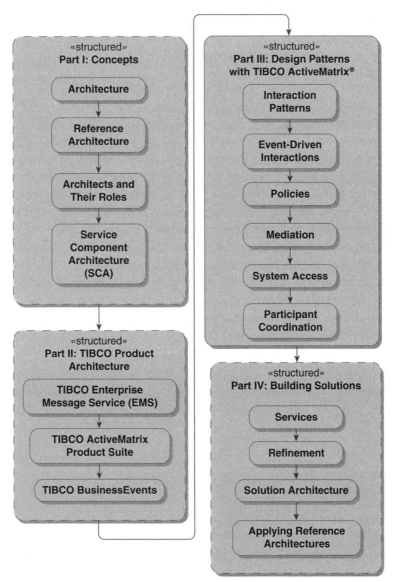

Figure P-3: *Book Structure*

this section are technology specific and detailed, getting into the product structure and architecture. Although the discussions are specific to the current version of the products (TIBCO Enterprise Message Service 6.x, TIBCO ActiveMatrix Service Bus and Service Grid 3.x, TIBCO

ActiveMatrix BusinessWorks 5.9, TIBCO ActiveMatrix BPM 1.x, and TIBCO BusinessEvents 4.x), most of the discussions will remain valid as these products evolve. Most product changes will result in augmentations rather than alterations.

Part III examines foundational design patterns: interactions between pairs of components, event-driven interactions, policies, mediation, external system access, and the coordination of activities. The discussions in this section are a mixture of technology-neutral design patterns and product-specific implementation choices for these patterns. Some discussions, particularly those surrounding policies, get quite detailed.

Part IV looks at building solutions, examining the concept of services, building solutions through the process of refinement, and applying reference architectures (design patterns). The discussions in this section are, once again, abstract (high level) and technology independent.

The book is intended to be read linearly, but there is some flexibility in this. Parts I and II can be read independently, but the discussions in Part III require an understanding of both prior parts. Part IV can be read after Part I, but the reader will find its discussion more compelling if Parts II and III have been read first.

Acknowledgments

Presenting material that touches on as many topics as this book does is, to say the least, challenging. This book series, and in fact the entire approach to presenting the material, would never have occurred without the persistent combination of challenge and encouragement provided by Michael Fallon, Madan Mashalkar, and Alan Brown over the past decade. Through them I have learned a great deal about both the challenges and techniques of knowledge transfer.

The design patterns presented in this book are a synthesis of the collective experience of the TIBCO global architects with whom I have worked over the years: Dave Ashton, Pong-Ning Ching, Richard Flather, Ben Gundry, Nochum Klein, Dave Leigh, Marco Malva, and Janet Strong. It is through their collaboration and the efforts of the other field architects that these patterns have been explored, refined, and tested.

I have received much support from TIBCO Software Inc. in the production of this book. For this I would like to thank Wen Miao, Paul Asmar, Jan Plutzer, and Murray Rode.

Many people reviewed the draft manuscript and provided valuable feedback. Comments from Bert Hooyman, Ignacio Silva-Lepe, and Lee Kleir led to significant improvements in the structure and content of the book. Feedback from Jose Carlos Estefania Aulet, Michael Blaha, Massimiliano Bonaveri, Antonio Bruno, Lloyd Fischer, Alex Garrison, Yuri Gogolitsyn, Jose Maria Lopez Higuera, Brian Hinsley, Alexandre Jeong, James Keegan, Joseph Meyer, Alexander Orsini, Mohan Sidda, Mark Shelton, and Moritz Weinrich helped to further refine the content. I thank you all for your support.

Finally, I would like to thank my wife, Maria, for supporting me in the writing of yet another book. Without her support, nothing is possible.

About the Author

 **Dr. Paul C. Brown** is a principal software architect at TIBCO Software Inc., author of *Succeeding with SOA: Realizing Business Value Through Total Architecture* (Addison-Wesley, 2007) and *Implementing SOA: Total Architecture In Practice* (Addison-Wesley, 2008), and a coauthor of the SOA Manifesto (soa-manifesto.org). His model-based tool architectures are the foundation of a diverse family of applications that design distributed control systems, process control interfaces, internal combustion engines, and NASA satellite missions. Dr. Brown's extensive design work on enterprise-scale information systems led him to develop the total architecture concept: Business processes and information systems are so intertwined that they must be architected together. Dr. Brown received his Ph.D. in computer science from Rensselaer Polytechnic Institute and his BSEE from Union College. He is a member of IEEE and ACM.

Part I

Concepts

The obvious is that which is never seen
until someone expresses it simply.
—K. Gibran

Chapter 1

The IT World
Is Evolving

From Systems to Processes

Business pressures are changing the way things are done in the IT world. The system-centric design focus of the past (Figure 1-1) is no longer sufficient for today's projects. The reason for this is that a narrow focus on individual systems leads to a proliferation of point-to-point interfaces. They are so specific in terms of implementation technology and information content that they are unusable in any other context. The resulting rat's nest of dedicated interfaces is brittle and· expensive to maintain. It impedes the enterprise's ability to respond to changing business conditions.

Service-oriented architecture (SOA) is based on the design concept that functionality can be packaged and made accessible in a way that allows common capabilities to be implemented once and shared widely.

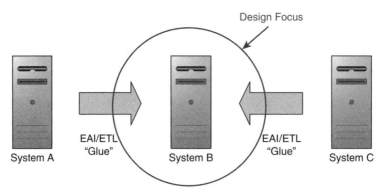

Figure 1-1: *System-Centric Design Focus*

Most services end up being wrappers around functionality that already resides in one or more existing systems. The service provides access to this functionality in a platform-neutral manner, thus facilitating the usability of the service.

Conceptualizing suitable services, however, requires an expanded design focus (Figure 1-2). Consideration of the service users as well as the service providers is required to ensure that the functionality is conveniently usable. Conceptualizing the service operations requires thinking about the capabilities of the systems providing the functionality and the needs of the systems utilizing the functionality. A failure to

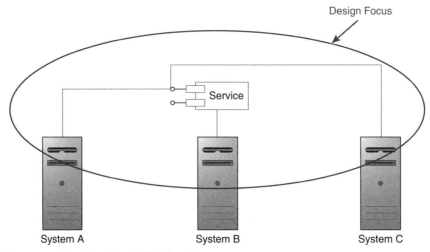

Figure 1-2: *Service-Centric Design Focus*

take the consumer needs into account yields services that are not well suited to the consumer. Such failures negate all of the potential SOA benefits.

Improving the business often requires optimizing a collaborative business process (Figure 1-3). In these processes the actual structure of the business process is not explicitly represented—it is implicit in the pattern of communications between the process participants. For example, the implicit process shown in Figure 1-3 starts when a user interface action invokes a service provided by System A, which invokes a service provided by System B, which ultimately invokes a service provided by System C. Improving such processes requires a design focus that encompasses all of the process participants and their interactions.

Business process management (BPM) seeks to further improve a business process through its explicit management (Figure 1-4). In contrast with collaborative business processes, a managed business process requires an explicit representation of the business process and the resources required to execute the process. The process manager then manages the process through a series of interactions with the process participants, generally some combination of both people and systems. This type of project requires a design focus that encompasses the process definition, the process manager, and all of the process participants.

What these examples illustrate is that the focus of IT projects is evolving away from system-centric design toward process-centric

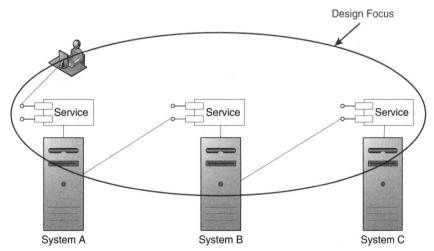

Figure 1-3: *Collaborative Business Process Design Focus*

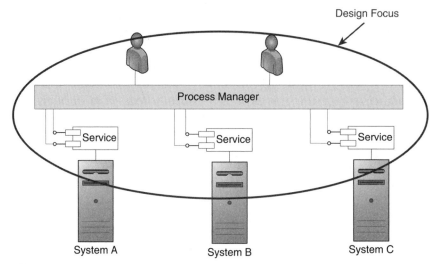

Figure 1-4: *Managed Business Process Design Focus*

design. This shift certainly makes sense from the perspective of business-IT alignment since business process improvements are what bring value to the enterprise. Process definitions provide the tangible connection between the business and IT. Whether a process defines an unmanaged collaboration or a managed orchestration, it precisely identifies the participants (both people and systems) and defines their required interactions. This perspective thus defines the requirements for each participant while ensuring that these requirements, collectively, provide business value.

Many business processes will extend beyond the boundaries of the enterprise to include customers, business partners, and regulatory agencies. These processes define the role of your enterprise in the larger ecosystem in which it participates. They define the interactions between your enterprise and external entities and, in so doing, define the requirements for external-facing system interfaces.

Whether processes are fully contained within the enterprise or extend beyond its borders, it is the process perspective that is required to conduct today's IT projects and keep them focused on delivering business value. But who assembles this perspective and relates it to the systems that are involved? The answer is the architect.

Architecture and Architects

When a design involves two or more participants (whether systems or organizations), the processes that define the required participants and their collaboration must be rationalized. The product of this effort is the solution architecture, and the responsibility for producing it belongs to the architect.

What actually comprises an architecture will be discussed in the chapters that follow, but for now we simply make an observation: It is amazing how infrequently projects consciously define their architectures. Ask yourself: Is there is anybody on your project team whose responsibility it is to define the business processes and identify the participants and their interactions? Does anybody evaluate this architecture in terms of its suitability for the task at hand? But before you answer these questions, take a look at the next few chapters to understand what we mean by architecture—you may be a bit surprised.

If the answer is no, then nobody is responsible for the overall architecture. Often you end up with an accidental architecture, the result of an accumulation of system-centric design decisions. This is the source of the chewing-gum-and-bailing-wire collection of systems that result in high IT maintenance costs and lengthy development projects.

The alternative, a well-considered architecture, is not just nice to have. As we shall see in Chapter 5, spending time on architecture consistently leads to shorter project durations—shorter by as much as 25%. You literally can't afford to ignore architecture.

There is, however, a challenge. Individual projects rarely (if ever) implement complete architectures. Instead, each project implements or modifies only a fragment of the enterprise architecture. It takes the accumulated results of multiple projects to realize the enterprise architecture.

Two distinct architecture roles emerge from this challenge: project architects and enterprise architects. Enterprise architects define the overall vision for the enterprise and guide the projects so that each contributes to achieving the vision. Their design scope is the entire enterprise. Project architects have a narrower scope: the portion of the enterprise architecture that is impacted by the present project. They are responsible for determining exactly what this scope is and making changes in a manner that is consistent with the enterprise architecture vision. Project and enterprise architects must obviously collaborate to achieve the enterprise architecture vision. Chapter 5 explores these two roles and their interactions in some detail.

Summary

As your approach to designing IT systems becomes more sophisticated, the perspective that governs the design has to evolve. Early designs focused largely on the needs of individual systems. Services force the perspective to expand to include the consumers of the services as well as the providers. Improving business processes requires a focus that includes all process participants, both people and systems, along with their interactions. Business process management requires an explicit model of the process as well as an understanding of how the process manager interacts with all of the process participants. This evolution reflects a shift in thinking away from system-centric designs and toward process-centric designs.

The responsibility for maintaining a perspective that includes the business process, along with the multiple systems and organizations involved in the process, belongs to the architect. But you don't build the enterprise's business processes and systems all at once: You build them piecemeal, one project at a time. This requires two variations of the architect's role. The enterprise architect keeps the complete picture in perspective and defines what the eventual enterprise architecture should be. The project architect looks more narrowly at the portion of the enterprise architecture being impacted by the current project. It is important that the enterprise architect guide the project architects to ensure that individual project design decisions are consistent with the enterprise architecture vision.

Let's start by taking a look at what we mean when we say architecture.

Chapter 2

The Scope of Total Architecture

When you look at business processes today, you are faced with two inescapable facts: First, the business process participants include both systems and people, and second, the business process design is so inextricably intertwined with the IT systems design that you cannot design them independently.

Taken together, these two facts argue for a comprehensive approach to architecture and design, one that encompasses both people and systems, and includes the processes that define their interactions and the information (and other artifacts) involved in the processes. We call this comprehensive approach *total architecture* (Figure 2-1).

Unfortunately, many project teams and enterprise architecture groups do not have anyone charged with the responsibility for this total architecture scope. Instead, they have many specialists: the business analysts responsible for process design; the managers and supervisors responsible for organizing the people involved in the process; the database administrators and data quality specialists responsible for the information involved in the process; and the application, service, infrastructure, and network architects responsible for various aspects of these systems. However, none of these are responsible for determining whether all these pieces fit together to successfully address the business purpose.

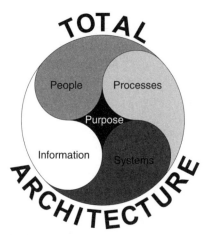

Figure 2-1: *Total Architecture Scope*

The consequence of not having anyone responsible for the total architecture is that often the pieces do not fit together particularly well, at least at first (Figure 2-2). The result is that rework is required to refine these so that they fit together properly by the time the project is completed. As we shall see in Chapter 5, without adequate consideration of architecture the resulting rework can double the duration of complex

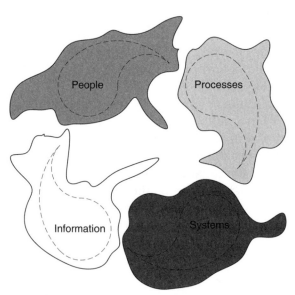

Figure 2-2: *Without the Total Architecture Perspective*

projects. With appropriate consideration of architecture the duration of these projects can be reduced by as much as 25%.

The first challenge presented by total architecture is simply keeping the big picture in perspective—understanding individual business processes and how those processes require people and systems to interact. We also need to understand how business processes interact with one another as each produces or consumes artifacts from other processes. Much of this interaction involves an exchange of information, so you need to know where information resides, and how and when the business processes require its movement.

Ideally, there is an individual—an architect—charged with the responsibility of keeping this all in focus and ensuring that the local decisions made concerning people (organizations), systems, information, and business processes are consistent across the board. Being effective in this role also requires some level of authority to adjust local decisions to ensure that they are consistent with the big picture.

The world, of course, is often less than ideal. In many circumstances there is no individual charged with maintaining the total architecture perspective. However, this does not render the perspective unimportant. Even if your personal responsibility is narrower in scope, the more you keep the total architecture in perspective the more you will be assured that your pieces, at least, will fit smoothly into the big picture.

Maintaining the total architecture perspective will also enable you to recognize when other pieces are not fitting well and raise the issue. Of course, since you don't have the overall authority to mandate change, you will have to "sell" the idea that the change is required. Take up the challenge, for this is a useful skill to have as an architect. You have to convince others that your architectural ideas will solve their problems anyway, so you might as well build your skills as you grow into that role.

Of course, simply saying that you need to consider all of the total architecture aspects doesn't tell you how do go about doing it. Let's take a look at how they all fit together to form an architecture.

Chapter 3

Aspects of Architecture

To many people the term architecture evokes images of box-and-line diagrams such as the one shown in Figure 3-1. This type of perspective is important as it shows the components and their communications channels, but it only tells part of the story. It does not, for example, tell you the nature of the work being performed nor does it tell you how the participants collaborate to perform that work.

The organization of the work and the collaboration of the participants in performing that work are also essential aspects of the architecture (Figure 3-2). In the IT world the work takes the form of processes. The picture is completed by mapping these processes onto the elements of the architecture pattern. In all but the most trivial of circumstances the architecture will involve more than one process, each of which is mapped onto the architecture pattern.

Process Models

Process models are just structures of activities that indicate both the activities being performed and the artifacts that are exchanged. In many cases these artifacts are simply data structures, but there may be physical artifacts as well such as goods and payments.

In the process model example shown in Figure 3-3 we see five activities. The first activity simply selects the work to follow, in this case the

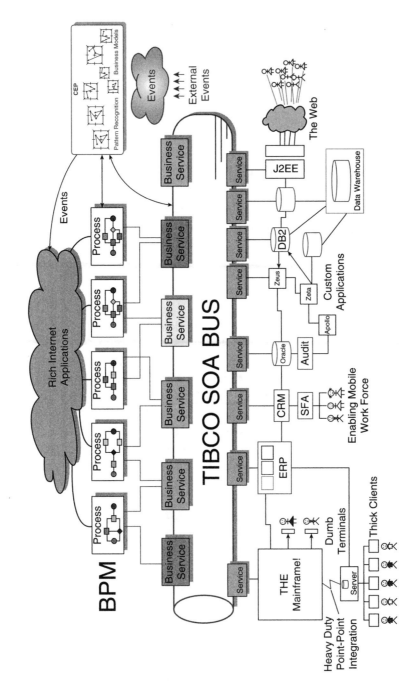

Figure 3-1: *Sketch of an Architecture Pattern*

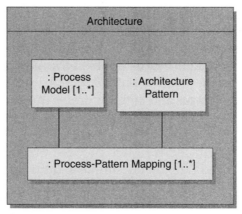

Figure 3-2: *Essential Aspects of an IT Architecture*

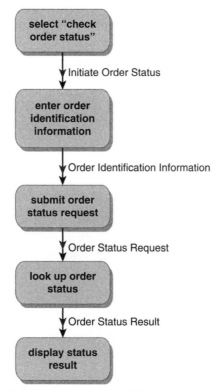

Figure 3-3: *Check Order Status Process Model*

checking of the order status. The interaction with the second activity involves a communication indicating that "check order status" has been selected. The second activity gathers the information needed to identify the order so that its status can be retrieved and communicates this information to the next activity. The third activity submits the request for the order status and communicates this request. The fourth activity executes the order status request and returns the order status result. The final activity displays the status result.

In most of the interactions in this process, the nature of the information being conveyed is relatively simple and the information content is implicit in the label given to the communications artifact in the diagram. But the term "order status result" is ambiguous: How much information does it actually convey? Such ambiguity makes it necessary to model the information content of the communication as an adjunct to the process model. Figure 3-4 shows some of the information that might be included in the result of this example. Note that the actual data structures are not being modeled—only their information content.

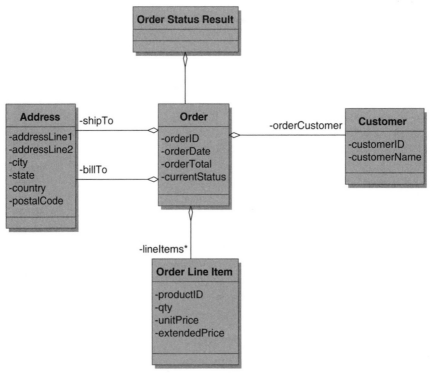

Figure 3-4: *Possible Information Content of an Order Status Result*

Architecture Patterns

The architecture pattern shows the structure of the participants in the process. It identifies the participants and the communication channels available between them. It also describes any constraints on the participants and communications channels.

Figure 3-5 is an example pattern found in many enterprises today. The customer (a person) interacts locally with a browser using keyboard and display. The browser interacts with Apache Tomcat application servers using HTTP over a WAN. The application server accesses services via SOAP over JMS, and these services are provided by TIBCO ActiveMatrix BusinessWorks™ implementations. The services access the back-end Order Management System via proprietary interfaces. In keeping with the total architecture concept, both people and systems are included in the architecture pattern.

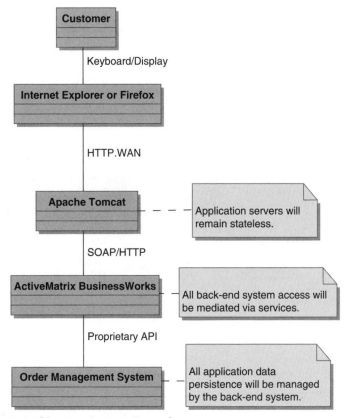

Figure 3-5: *Architecture Pattern Example*

As part of the architecture pattern it is appropriate to indicate constraints on the roles that the participants can play. The example shows three such constraints: Application servers will remain stateless; access to back-end systems will be mediated via services; and application data persistence will be managed by the back-end systems.

Process-Pattern Mapping

Mapping the process model onto the architecture pattern involves making design decisions about which participants will perform which activities in the process. The example of Figure 3-6 uses a UML Activity Diagram to show the mapping. Each of the diagram's swimlanes represents one of the process participants. The process activities are then overlaid on the swimlanes, thus indicating which of the participants is

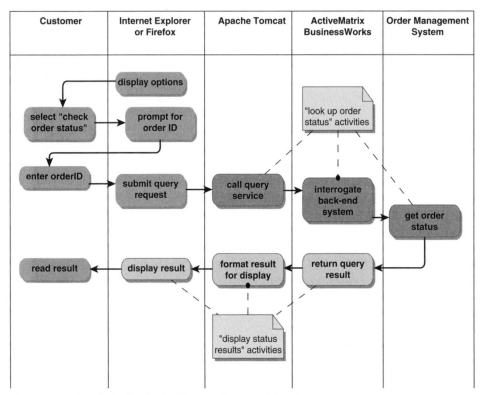

Figure 3-6: *Check Order Status Process-Pattern Mapping*

responsible for which of the activities. Interactions between activities assigned to different participants indicate the need for those participants to interact and thus indicate the need for interfaces.

One of the interesting things that occurs in mapping the process activities onto the participants is that some process activities become distributed across multiple participants. In this example, the "lookup order status" activity becomes three activities distributed across Apache Tomcat, ActiveMatrix BusinessWorks™, and the Order Management System. Similarly the "display status results" becomes three activities distributed across ActiveMatrix BusinessWorks, Apache Tomcat, and the browser.

Why Should You Care about Architecture?

It is appropriate to ask why you should care about architecture. The reality is that real-world processes and patterns are complex, and there are many ways in which the process models can be mapped onto the architecture patterns. These mappings reflect design decisions: Which participants should be responsible for each activity? Which activities should be distributed across multiple participants and how? Which communications channels should be used for each interaction?

Even with the best architecture pattern, an inappropriate mapping can lead to a show-stopping failure—one that will require major rework. The goal of mapping the process onto the pattern is to make the mapping explicit so that it can be examined, reviewed, and refined while it is still a paper design. Changes at this stage are inexpensive and easily accommodated.

This mapping has to be done anyway at some point to complete the design, and you also need to do the mapping to evaluate the adequacy of the architecture pattern. The only real question is when to do the mapping. As we shall see in Chapter 5, evidence from real projects shows that doing the mapping early in the project can reduce overall project duration by as much as 25%. The larger and more complex the project, the bigger the impact that architecture has upon project duration.

It is important to record the mapping: Draw the picture and save it. All too often the mapping is done verbally: The architecture pattern is displayed and someone talks through how the process is executed by the participants in the pattern. Unfortunately, the only people who will understand the mapping are those who participated in the discussion, and likely that understanding will be incomplete. What you lose with this approach is the ability to share the mapping with others. Architects who did not participate in the discussion will be unable to learn, review, and comment. Businesspeople will not be able to review and validate the proposed process execution. Designers and developers will not fully understand how their components are expected to participate in the process.

An ATM Architecture Example

Since the query example was relatively simple, let's take a look at a richer architecture, this time of a banking system involving an automated teller machine (ATM). This architecture (Figure 3-7) involves four different process models (withdraw cash, make deposit, check balance, and transfer funds) all mapped onto the same architecture pattern.

ATM Architecture Pattern

The architecture pattern for this example (Figure 3-8) is relatively simple. The ATM System comprises two types of components: ATM Machines and an ATM Server. The remaining components are the people (customers) who use the ATM service and the Bank Systems that actually manage the account balances.

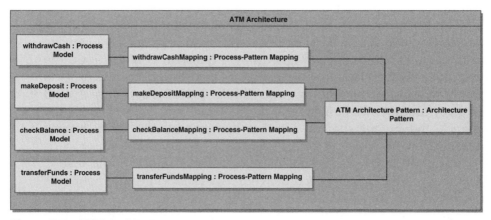

Figure 3-7: *ATM Architecture*

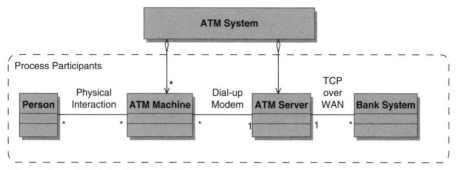

Figure 3-8: *ATM Architecture Pattern*

ATM Withdraw Cash Process Model

There are four processes executed in this architecture. One of these is the withdraw cash process illustrated in Figure 3-9. The figure shows the sunny-day scenario for this process. This particular depiction of the process is not necessarily specific to the ATM approach and describes equally well an interaction with a human teller, albeit with some differences in the artifacts involved.

The withdraw cash process begins with the customer presenting credentials (e.g., the ATM card) and some form of identification (e.g., the PIN number). The first activity authenticates the customer using some reference information that indicates the acceptable associations between credentials and identification. Next, the account is identified and the authorization of the customer to access the account is established. The availability of funds is established and, if available, the funds are disbursed to the customer. The process concludes with the account balance being updated and a receipt being given to the customer.

Beyond the structuring of the activities, the process indicates the inputs required for each activity and the results that are produced. The inputs and results are important because they generally indicate the need for interactions with other business processes and their supporting systems. Interactions often require effort to implement, and thus recognizing the need for such interactions clarifies the true scope of the project.

This process model is, of course, incomplete, for it does not show what happens if the funds turn out to be unavailable or if the funds are not disbursed successfully. In a real architecture, these and other

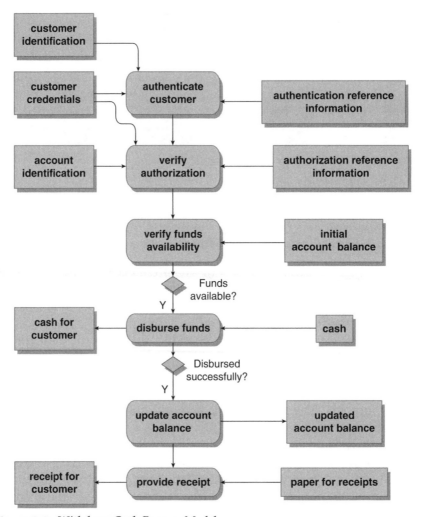

Figure 3-9: *Withdraw Cash Process Model*

alternate scenarios would have to be detailed from a business process perspective.

The sequencing of activities in the process model should be carefully considered. If the process model shows a specific sequence of activities, as in Figure 3-9, someone implementing that process would have no choice other than to execute those activities in that specific sequence.

To allow maximum flexibility in implementing processes it is important to indicate where activities can be done in parallel. Figure 3-10 shows a hypothetical restructuring of the withdraw cash process to show allowed parallelism. This process indicates that the activities of authentication, authorization, and verifying funds availability could be performed in parallel. Similarly, it indicates that the printing of the receipt and the updating of the account balance could be done concurrently.

Showing activities in parallel provides the maximum flexibility when implementing the process. The designer is now aware that

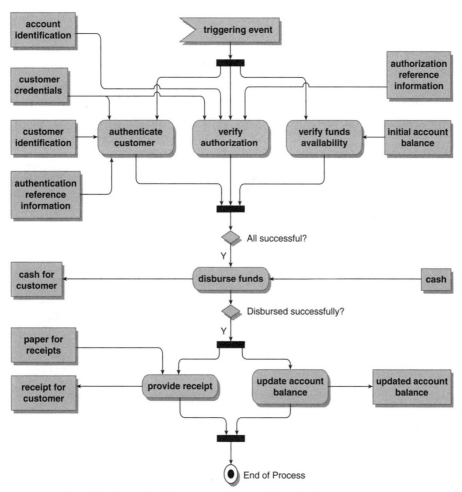

Figure 3-10: *Withdraw Cash Process Model with Parallelization*

certain activities could be performed simultaneously to minimize latency in the process. On the other hand, a sequential execution of the activities shown earlier is also perfectly acceptable.

ATM Withdraw Cash Process-Pattern Mapping

The mapping of the withdraw cash process onto the ATM architecture pattern is shown in Figure 3-11. As in the earlier example, some of the activities become distributed across multiple participants. In this particular case, the distribution itself introduces some exception scenarios that require some refinement of the process. One particular scenario of concern is when there might be a delay between the verification of funds availability and the reporting of the funds distribution. The problem to be avoided here is one of the funds still appearing to be available in the bank system and being withdrawn (via some unspecified mechanism) before the account balance can be updated.

The solution to this problem is a refinement of the "verify funds availability" activity into one that obtains a disbursal authorization. This disbursal authorization places a hold on the funds in the account

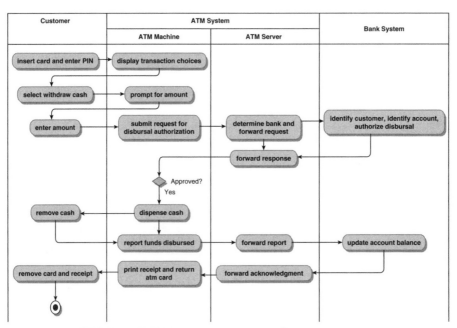

Figure 3-11: *Withdraw Cash Process-Pattern Mapping*

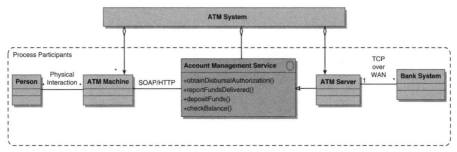

Figure 3-12: *ATM Architecture Pattern with Services*

and authorizes the funds to be delivered to the customer within some specified time period. This dialog involves the return of an authorization number with the authorization and the requirement to supply this same authorization number when the funds disbursal is reported. At that time the hold on the funds is removed and the account is debited by the amount actually delivered.

The example in Figure 3-11 illustrates the kind of design problem that can arise as the process is mapped onto the architecture pattern. Explicitly modeling the mapping affords the opportunity to not only identify the design problem but also modify the design to address the issue.

ATM Architecture Example with Services

Designs involving services can be readily represented in the same manner. The starting point is updating the architecture pattern to indicate where services come into play (Figure 3-12). In this example the Account Management Service has been added with the ATM Server providing the service implementation and the ATM Machine using the services.

Simply adding the service to the architecture pattern does not indicate how the service operations participate in the process. That information is added as the process is mapped onto the architecture pattern. Figure 3-13 shows the process-pattern mapping modified to indicate which service operations are being invoked.

Augmenting the mapping to show where process operations occur provides a lot of useful information. It shows both what happens behind the scenes when the operation is invoked and how the operation supports the larger business process. Both perspectives are

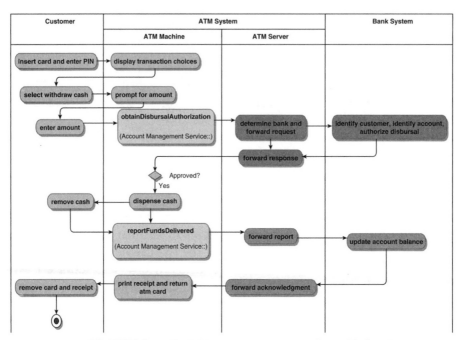

Figure 3-13: *ATM Withdraw Cash Process-Pattern Mapping with Services*

essential to validate that the service operations can adequately support their intended utilization. Furthermore, if there are expectations of reuse for service operations, the mappings of other business processes should be able to use the same operations. For example, a funds transfer can be assembled from an obtainDisbursalAuthorization and reportFundsDelivered on one account along with a depositFunds on a second account.

Summary

There are three essential aspects to an architecture: the architecture pattern, one or more process models, and the mappings of those process models onto the architecture pattern. The architecture pattern shows the participants in the process, the communications channels between them, and the constraints on their usage. Each process model shows how a particular kind of work is organized and the artifacts (information and physical entities) involved in performing that work.

The process-pattern mapping shows how the participants in the process carry out the work of the process.

The mapping of the process activities onto the process participants provides many advantages:

- It surfaces many design decisions and makes their resolution explicit. When individual activities are performed by a single participant, the mapping indicates the participant.

- When one activity provides inputs to another and these activities are assigned to different participants, the mapping indicates the need for the two participants to interact—and the need for an interface!

- When an activity becomes split across several participants, the mapping indicates the detailed responsibilities of each participant along with the need for interactions between them.

- Analyzing the mapping allows you to identify bottlenecks and determine where load distribution will be required.

- The mapping enables a detailed examination of failure modes (the loss of individual participants and individual interactions), which may motivate a modification to the process to better handle the failures.

Documenting the full architecture, including the process-pattern mapping, is important. It makes the architecture explicit so that it can be readily examined and critiqued by other architects. It affords an opportunity for stakeholders (businesspeople, in particular) to validate the process definitions and verify that the proposed implementation is suitable for their needs. Finally, it helps the designers responsible for the individual participants clearly understand their design requirements, including the role that their components play in the larger design.

Architecture documentation clarifies the roles that services are expected to play in a design. It shows how service operations participate in business processes, which are the ultimate source of their requirements. It shows the internal architecture of the services, a perspective that is essential in verifying the service operation's ability to support the business process. And finally, it affords the opportunity to establish the potential for reuse: the participation of the same service operation in two or more processes.

Chapter 4

Reference Architecture

The architecture of an enterprise can involve hundreds or thousands of processes that play out against the enterprise's architecture pattern. Documenting each of these processes individually can be a daunting task. However, it is commonplace for many processes to follow similar patterns: The work has a similar structure and this structure is mapped consistently onto the architecture pattern. In such cases these processes can be documented by capturing their common pattern in a *reference architecture*.

Comparing the architecture of one enterprise against the architecture of another can be similarly complex. The details of individual processes and architecture patterns are frequently different, yet often their structure is similar. Once again the similar structure can be captured and shared in the form of a reference architecture.

So what is a reference architecture? It is simply an abstracted architecture (Figure 4-1). The reference process model shows the abstracted structure of the work process. The reference architecture pattern shows the abstracted structure of the process participants.[1] The process-pattern mapping shows how the abstracted process maps onto the abstracted architecture pattern.

---

1. Bass et al. refer to the reference process model as simply the reference model and the reference architecture pattern as simply the architecture pattern. Len Bass, Paul Clements, and Rick Kazman, *Software Architecture in Practice, Second Edition*, Boston: Addison-Wesley (2007).

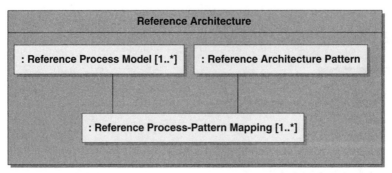

Figure 4-1: *Essential Aspects of an IT Reference Architecture*

Reference Process Model

The reference process model is an abstracted version of the process. Figure 4-2, for example, is an abstracted version of the process shown in Figure 3-3. The abstracted process has exactly the same structure as

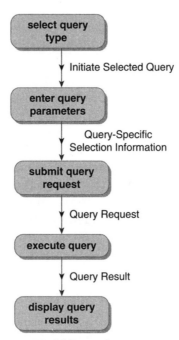

Figure 4-2: *Reference Process Model Example*

the more detailed model, and the artifacts that are passed are abstractions of the artifacts passed in the more detailed model. This similarity of structure is an essential element of the reference process model. The similarity ensures that reasoning about the reference model also applies to the more detailed models.

Reference Architecture Pattern

The reference architecture pattern is an abstraction of the architecture pattern. For example, Figure 4-3 is an abstracted version of the architecture pattern shown in Figure 3-5. Note that the structure is exactly the same. Structural similarity is an essential requirement both in abstracting

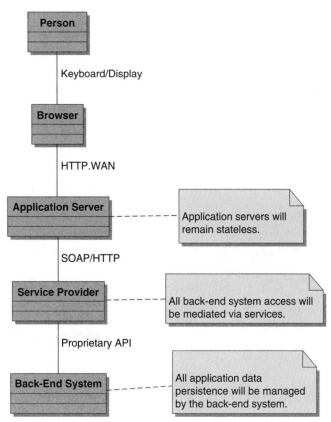

Figure 4-3: *Reference Architecture Pattern Example*

a reference architecture pattern and in creating an actual architecture pattern from a reference architecture pattern.

Reference Process-Pattern Mapping

The process-pattern mapping for the reference architecture (Figure 4-4) is what you would expect: a mapping of the reference process model onto the reference architecture pattern. The mapping makes clear which participants are responsible for which activities and, when activities are split across multiple participants, the roles of those individual participants. Once again, the structure must be the same as that of the mapping being abstracted.

Applications of Reference Architectures

Reference architectures abstract common features from ordinary architectures. In so doing, they provide a means of showing common structure across these architectures. This can be useful in a number of circumstances:

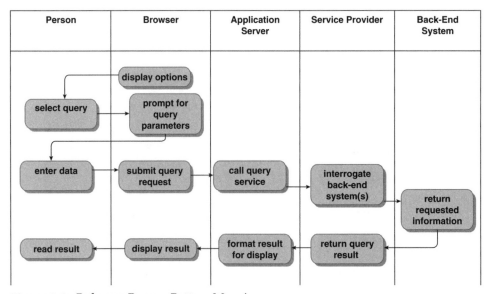

Figure 4-4: *Reference Process-Pattern Mapping*

- Simplifying the documentation of a number of processes that all share a common structure and are mapped onto a common architecture pattern. The reference architecture allows a single process model and a single mapping to document the collection of processes with the same structure.

- Sharing a design pattern across different architectures. In these cases the reference architecture captures the common work structure and an abstracted architecture pattern.

- Specifying the preferred approach to solving a particular kind of problem. In these cases the reference architecture captures the work structure common to solving the problem and illustrates how the work structure should be mapped onto a particular architecture pattern.

This last circumstance is an important one in the enterprise, for it provides a means for enterprise architects to communicate preferred approaches to project architects. In these cases the architecture pattern is typically quite specific, indicating the actual types of components required within the enterprise. In contrast, the process model is more abstract, covering a family of processes with similar structure. For example, the enterprise architects may wish to specify how queries (Figure 4-2) should be performed with the enterprise's preferred architecture pattern (Figure 3-5). The resulting mapping would look like Figure 4-5, mapping a generic process onto a specific architecture pattern.

Summary

A reference architecture is an abstracted version of an architecture. It has the same structure as an architecture, with process models, an architecture pattern, and a mapping of each process model onto the architecture pattern. The difference is that each process model depicts the abstracted structure of a set of actual processes and the architecture pattern depicts a (possibly) abstracted structure of the participants and their communications channels.

Because reference architectures abstract structure, they provide a convenient means of communicating structure without having to be tied down to specifics. They are useful for summarizing the structure of

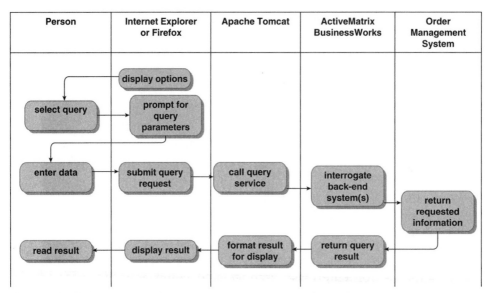

Figure 4-5: *Reference Architecture Mapping with a Specific Architecture Pattern*

related processes, comparing structure between different architectures, and communicating preferred design patterns.

Chapter 5

Architects and Their Roles

Business Processes and Organizational Silos

Business processes frequently span multiple systems and their organizational silos (Figure 5-1). In the past, most projects making changes to these business processes have tended to focus on individual activities associated with a single application silo. The design focus for these projects was system-centric. Later, another project would tackle another activity, and so on. For the most part, business processes evolved incrementally through a succession of system-focused projects.

This picture, however, has changed. These days, projects often need to make coordinated changes to multiple systems. One driver for this is the demand for larger-scale improvements to business processes, such as shrinking the overall time frame for process execution. Another driver is the introduction of new architectural styles such as service-oriented architecture (SOA) and business process management (BPM). Services are often new abstracted interfaces wrapped around the functionality of existing systems. Business process management introduces a process coordinator to direct the activities of both people and systems. SOA and BPM projects thus involve coordinated changes to multiple systems. And this presents a challenge.

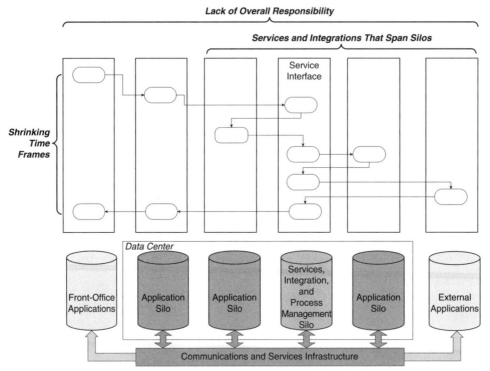

Figure 5-1: *Business Processes and Organizational Silos*

Development Processes

When projects focus on changes to a single system, the development process is fairly simple (Figure 5-2). The requirements are assembled and given to the development team responsible for the system. The development team determines the required changes and implements them. The result is run through quality assurance (QA) and then placed in production.

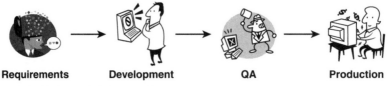

Figure 5-2: *System-Centric Development*

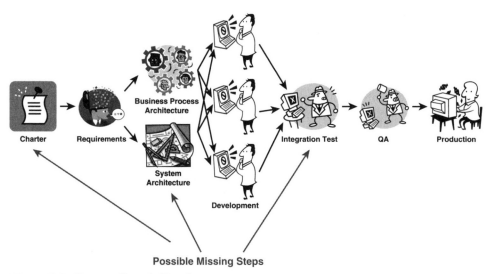

Figure 5-3: *Process-Centric Development*

This type of development process may be adequate for making changes to a single system, but it is deficient when it comes to making coordinated changes to multiple systems. For that you need the kind of process-centric development shown in Figure 5-3. The key difference is the reintroduction of a conscious architecture step into the process. We say reintroduction because classical software engineering has always had an architecture step here. However, in many development shops this step has atrophied to the point where it no longer exists. If so, it needs to be reintroduced.

For those of you working with agile development, you need to pay particular attention to the manner in which architecture is addressed in your development process. It is all too easy to focus only on the needs of the current build (scrum) when it comes to making architecture decisions. The decisions you make, and the development investment in implementing those decisions, can back you into a corner later on when you encounter more complex architectural challenges. Make sure that you keep the downstream architectural challenges in focus when you make your design decisions. For a more detailed discussion of the issues and tradeoffs, see Boehm and Turner's *Balancing Agility and Discipline: A Guide for the Perplexed.*[1]

---

1. Barry Boehm and Richard Turner, *Balancing Agility and Discipline: A Guide for the Perplexed*, Boston: Addison-Wesley (2004).

The Architecture Step

So what's going on in this architecture step? It is simply the examination of the end-to-end business process along with the end-to-end system dialog that supports it, rationalizing the changes that are required, and then determining what changes need to be made to individual organizations and systems. The architects are leading the development process and determining what each of the development teams needs to do.

The total architecture synthesis methodology described in *Implementing SOA*[2] describes a comprehensive and efficient approach to developing an architecture in far more detail than can be covered here. Nevertheless, it is worth standing back and getting a feel for the kinds of decisions that an architect typically faces.

Figure 5-4 illustrates some of the questions that might arise in a service-oriented architecture. If a service is expected to provide functionality to different front-end systems, the architect needs to consider

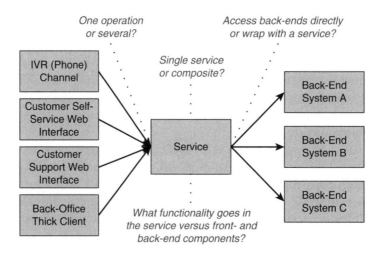

Figure 5-4: *Architectural Decisions*

2. Paul C. Brown, *Implementing SOA: Total Architecture in Practice*, Boston: Addison-Wesley (2008).

whether a single operation can support the multiple front-end systems. When back-end systems need to be accessed, should the service directly access the systems via their proprietary interfaces, or should those interfaces themselves be wrapped with services? Should the service be a monolith, or should it, in turn, be composed of other services?

But the most telling question is what functionality belongs in the front-end systems versus the service versus the back-end systems. It is in considering this question that the full scope of architecture responsibility becomes apparent, for this question cannot be answered from the perspective of a single system or service. It requires an overview of the full set of business process participants.

For historical reasons, the question of where functionality belongs is particularly important. Prior to service-oriented architectures, most front-end systems interacted directly with back-end systems. The front-end systems ended up containing a mixture of two types of logic. One type of logic dealt with managing the interface and the other type dealt with managing the business process. The presence of business logic complicated the addition of new interfaces, for the business logic needed to be replicated. The presence of multiple interfaces complicated the maintenance of business logic, for it needed to be updated in multiple front-end systems.

Introducing a service layer or a business process manager affords the opportunity to improve the situation by moving the business process logic out of the front-end systems into shared services or business process models. The resulting division of responsibilities is similar to that found in the old IBM 3270 green-screen interfaces. The 3270 presented a collection of fields to be filled in and managed the navigation through these fields. The user filled in the fields and, when done, pressed a "do it" key. At this point the 3270 gathered all the data and submitted it to a back-end transaction that executed the business logic. Replicating this kind of separation of responsibilities between the front-end systems and the services or business processes that lie underneath can significantly simplify the evolution of the enterprise architecture.

However, it is important for you to recognize that this architecture pattern only affords the *opportunity* to separate interface and business process logic. Someone (namely the architect) must take advantage of this opportunity in order for the enterprise to realize the benefits. This should be done proactively, defining the roles and responsibilities of the front-end systems and the individual services as well as defining the interfaces between them before investing in the design of those systems and services.

The Architect as Policeman: An Anti-Pattern

Proactive architectural leadership is important. There is an alternate approach that is, unfortunately, a common architectural practice that ought to be avoided. In this alternate approach, architects police the design without leading it. The design is worked out collaboratively by the development teams—none of which is responsible for the overall business process and systems architecture. Only after the design has started to gel is it reviewed by the architects. *The problem with this model is that any changes suggested by the architects at this point require rework on the part of the development teams.* As we shall see in a moment, this rework can easily double the duration of a complex project. The policeman approach is thus to be avoided.

The Project Charter

The project charter can have a significant impact on the success of the project. This charter should address three key issues:

1. Quantifying business expectations
2. Establishing cost and schedule expectations
3. Quantifying business process risk

Quantifying Business Expectations

It is good practice to challenge the business to quantify their expectations regarding the project. Ask them directly how they are going to measure success. The answer brings focus to the design effort and can radically alter the architecture.

Consider a project that seeks to improve the productivity of the people involved in the business process. But by how much? A 5% productivity improvement requires automating some of the busywork that consumes people's time. A 50% productivity improvement will require automating half the work that people currently do. A 95% productivity improvement calls for completely automating the process and using the few remaining people for exception handling.

As this illustrates, the quantification of expectations can have a significant impact on the approach taken to the architecture and design. Consequently, it is a good practice to not only quantify the expectations but also build the measurements into the revised business process. The measurements will establish how successful the project was in achieving the goals and indicate whether further work is warranted.

Establishing Cost and Schedule Expectations

It is important to clearly understand the business expectations regarding the project cost and schedule right from the beginning, and it is equally important to understand what these represent. We have all heard project teams complain on day one of the project, "Where did those estimates come from?" This reflects a serious misunderstanding. Although the cost and schedule numbers may have started out as estimates, by the time the project is chartered they represent business expectations that the quantified business benefits can be achieved within the project's cost and schedule guidelines.

The import is that the first task of the architects should be to determine whether the quantified business benefits can, indeed, be achieved within the cost and schedule guidelines. This determination should be made as quickly and efficiently as possible so that if the answer is no, the bulk of the time and resources are left unspent. This affords maximum flexibility to the business in deciding what to do next, whether it is altering the project scope, adding time and resources, or cancelling the project and applying the resources to achieving other goals. The total architecture synthesis (TAS) methodology described *Implementing SOA*[3] provides an efficient approach that answers this question with minimal time and resources.

Quantifying Business Process Risks

The third key understanding required from the project charter is that of risk to the business. Not risk associated with the present project, but rather risk associated with the business processes that are impacted by the project. In particular, you want to understand two things:

- What is the business impact if a single execution of the business process fails?
- What is the business impact if the business process becomes unavailable for some period of time?

---

3. Paul C. Brown, *Implementing SOA: Total Architecture in Practice*, Boston: Addison-Wesley (2008).

Understanding these risks helps the architects to determine where business continuity is an issue. This is important because the techniques used to establish business continuity (fault tolerance, high availability, and site disaster recovery) significantly increase the cost of the resulting systems. A fully fault-tolerant, site-disaster-recovery-enabled solution will require a minimum of a four-fold increase in hardware and software over simply implementing the required business functionality. Such investments should only be undertaken when there is appropriate business justification. A more detailed discussion of business risks can be found in *Succeeding with SOA*.[4]

The Integration Test Step

The third step that may be missing from your present development process is that of systems integration. Although it is common practice in a system-centric design to simply deploy the changes and begin testing, this type of approach for a distributed system can lead to chaos. The reason is that it is often difficult to determine the source of a problem in a distributed system.

The system integration test step is nothing more than a well-thought-out order of assembly for the elements of the distributed system. Put parts A and B together and make sure they are communicating properly. Then add parts C and D and make sure they are talking properly. Continue adding parts incrementally until the entire solution is functioning on some basic level. Then begin more advanced testing.

This integration test step sounds so simple that you may be asking yourself why it is such a big deal. The answer is that in large-scale enterprise systems the time differential between spending a few days on a well-considered integration process and simply turning everything on at once can be as extreme as several months. It's well worth the effort.

Architecture Improves Project Schedules

Architecture isn't just a nice thing to do. It has a measurable impact on the duration of projects. Figure 5-5 presents a summary of data from

---

4. Paul C. Brown, *Succeeding with SOA: Realizing Business Value Through Total Architecture*, Boston: Addison-Wesley (2007).

160 projects showing the impact of architecture and risk resolution (architecture analysis) on the amount of rework that occurs in a project. There are three sets of curves on the graph, one representing data from

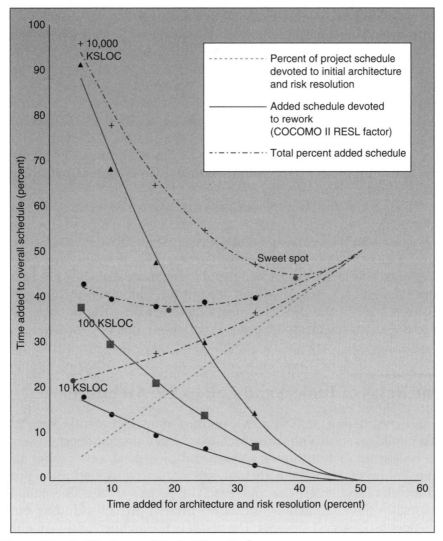

Figure 5-5: *Architecture and Project Duration*[5]

---

5. Barry Boehm, "Making a Difference in the Software Century," *Computer*, IEEE, March 2008, pp. 32–38. Used by permission. The data upon which the graph is based can be found in Appendix E of Barry Boehm and Richard Turner's *Balancing Agility and Discipline: A Guide for the Perplexed*, Boston: Addison-Wesley (2004).

small projects (10K lines of code), medium projects (100K lines of code), and very large projects (10 million lines of code). If you think about it, your enterprise architecture comprises a large-scale system of systems whose total complexity likely exceeds this very large project threshold by a wide margin. Projects that seek to make significant changes to the enterprise architecture are likely to be in this very large category.

So what is this graph telling us? It says that in large projects, with little or no architecture effort, the time added to the project for rework approaches 100%—doubling the duration of the project. It also shows that as time is added to the project for architecture, the amount of rework plummets. This effect is so dramatic that adding 40% for architecture reduces the time spent doing rework to 5% or so. Combining the time added for architecture with this small amount of rework gives us a 50% reduction in the time added to the project and a net 25% reduction in overall project duration. Architecture isn't just nice to have—it has real measurable benefits.

The fact that architecture work can have such a dramatic impact on project duration makes common sense. You are defining and then analyzing your high-level design while it is largely a paper exercise, doing development work only in controlled experiments to resolve feasibility questions. You're making, finding, and fixing mistakes while it is still a paper design and easily modified. In contrast, finding and fixing these mistakes later in the project requires more rework. The moral is: Do your due diligence on architecture. It will more than pay for itself.

The Roles of Project and Enterprise Architects

When considering architecture, one important fact stands out: You don't build an entire enterprise architecture in a single project. Instead, the enterprise architecture is constructed piecemeal, one project at a time. For this reason, there are two important architectural roles: project architect and enterprise architect. The project architect's role is to rationalize the total architecture of the present project including both business process and systems. The result is the architectural vision for what this particular project needs to build. The enterprise architect establishes the architecture vision for the enterprise and guides individual projects to contribute to realizing that vision. Creating and sharing architecture vision is critical to both roles.

Project Architect Responsibilities

The project architect is responsible for defining and communicating the overall architecture of the project's work—the big-picture design. This includes:

- Defining the end-to-end business process and supporting systems dialog
- Identifying and applying appropriate reference architectures
- Identifying existing services that can be used and incorporating them into the design
- Identifying opportunities for new services and engaging enterprise architects to qualify those opportunities and, where appropriate, specify the new services

Defining the End-to-End Business Process and Systems Dialog

The primary responsibility of the project architect is to define the changes to the business process and systems dialog required by the current project. Doing this requires understanding the present end-to-end business processes that are impacted and the end-to-end system dialogs that support them. Given this perspective, the changes required to achieve the project goals are defined and the specific changes required to each of the involved systems are identified.

An important aspect of this responsibility is documenting the business process and systems architecture so that it can be understood and reviewed by the other stakeholders in the project. This affords the business community the opportunity to review and validate the proposed changes before the design proceeds any further. It also helps the design teams responsible for the individual systems clearly understand the requirements for their particular systems and how they fit into the overall picture. The techniques described in Chapter 3 are central to this communication.

Identifying and Applying Reference Architectures

A challenging aspect of project architecture is to ensure that the project architecture contributes to the realization of the enterprise architecture vision. An important instrument in this endeavor is the reference architecture. Enterprise architects create reference architectures to illustrate how specific patterns of work should be implemented in the intended enterprise architecture.

The project architect's responsibility in this regard is to recognize the work patterns found in the current project and identify the appropriate reference architectures to be applied. An equally important responsibility is to determine when there are work patterns for which there are no reference architectures at present. If these work patterns appear likely to be found again, then the enterprise architects should be engaged to define the appropriate reference architecture.

Identifying and Applying Existing Services

Realizing the benefits of a service-oriented architecture requires re-using existing services, where appropriate, to avoid building unnecessary interfaces. This requires the project architect to examine the business processes impacted by the project, determine whether there are existing services that could be used, and incorporate those services into the architecture.

This exercise frequently requires a bit of creativity. Often the existing service will not fit cleanly into the initial conceptualization of the business process. Here the architect must experiment with the business process definition to determine whether a variation can be found that will both satisfy the business requirements and allow the use of the existing service operations. Failing that, the architect should consider whether a new or modified service operation would be appropriate. The enterprise architects should be engaged in this latter discussion.

Identifying New Service Opportunities

The project architect is in an ideal position to identify new service opportunities. This typically occurs when the project architect identifies functionality that looks like it might be usable in other contexts. However, it is typically beyond the charter of the project to validate the applicability of the proposed service in those other contexts. For that, the enterprise architects must be engaged and their involvement continued through the specification of the service. After that, the project team can implement the service as just another component of the project.

Enterprise Architect Responsibilities

The responsibilities of the enterprise architect are broad, and encompass:

- Defining the target architecture for the enterprise
- Defining a practical evolution strategy
- Defining reference architecture(s) consistent with the target architecture
- Guiding project teams in evolving toward the enterprise architecture
- Participating directly in projects requiring complex designs
- Training and mentoring project architects

Defining the Target Architecture for the Enterprise

The primary responsibility for the enterprise architect is to define the target architecture for the enterprise. This effort requires understanding the business drivers for the enterprise and determining the architecture changes required to be responsive to the business needs. Beyond simply defining the target architecture, the enterprise architects must articulate the manner in which the architecture changes contribute to the enterprise's ability to respond to business conditions.

Communicating this architecture vision is as important as defining it. In reality, the architecture will be realized through incremental changes being made by individual projects. Thus it is important that the project teams understand the rationale behind the architecture vision so that they can incorporate this thinking into their day-to-day decisions.

Defining a Practical Evolution Strategy

No matter how wonderful the new architecture vision, the reality is that the business is presently operating with the old architecture and must continue to operate during the transition. Thus it is important for the enterprise architects to define a practical, affordable migration strategy that keeps the enterprise operating during the transition. This is often a bigger challenge than defining the new architecture.

For example, the enterprise may settle on a service-oriented architecture, but on the first day there are no services. What is a project to do? It is unlikely that the project, if it is to justify its investment in terms of returned business benefit, will be able to afford to build every service it can identify. In such cases the enterprise architects must provide guidelines for determining which services should actually be built.

Defining Reference Architecture(s) Consistent with the Target Architecture

Enterprise architectures often focus on the architecture pattern—the arrangement of components, the communications channels between them, and the guidelines governing their use. However, this alone is not sufficient to guide project architects in the appropriate implementation of this architecture. There are many ways in which work functionality can be mapped onto the architecture pattern. Some of these are good and others are bad.

The purpose of a reference architecture is to define how a work process should be mapped onto an architecture pattern. Whether reference architecture is organized as one reference architecture, mapping many different work processes onto a single architecture pattern or as a series of reference architectures each mapping a single work process onto a subset of the overall architecture pattern, reference architecture serves to illustrate, by abstract example, the intended use of the architecture pattern.

Enterprise architects must pay attention to how closely their reference architectures meet the needs of the individual projects. Do the reference architectures match the work processes being found by the projects? Are they, in fact, being applied? Are there common work processes for which reference architectures have not yet been defined? Paying attention to the usage of reference architectures is one way to ensure that the architecture vision is appropriately realized and delivers value to the enterprise.

Guiding Project Teams in Evolving toward the Enterprise Architecture

Regardless of the quality of documentation surrounding the architecture vision and the reference architectures, there are always situations in which some interpretation is required to apply the vision to the problem at hand. Enterprise architects must be prepared to provide leadership to projects in such circumstances. The alternative, reviewing project-level designs after the fact, is a recipe for rework and project delay. Worst case, the architecture guidelines will be set aside because the degree of rework, and delay cannot be tolerated. There is no substitute for proactive leadership when it comes to architecture!

Directly Participating in Projects Requiring Complex Designs

This is sort of an extension of the previous point. When you encounter complex design situations that are not covered by existing reference architectures it may be far from obvious how the enterprise architecture vision can be applied to the situation. In such cases the most senior architects (namely the enterprise architects) should step in and assess the situation. It is, after all, their vision, and they are in the best position to determine how the present situation should be addressed.

One of two outcomes (or maybe a combination) will emerge from this situation: an architecture (and possibly a reference architecture) that describes the solution in a manner consistent with the present enterprise architecture vision, or a modified enterprise architecture vision that now encompasses the situation presented by the current project. Either way, it is important that the visionaries (namely the enterprise architects) be the ones deciding which route to take.

Train and Mentor Project Architects

Good architects don't grow on trees: They must be trained and groomed for the role. This is particularly true at the project level. Here you will find individuals from the technical side who are interested in higher-level design (i.e., architecture) but may not have the familiarity with business processes required for a balanced total architecture approach. Similarly, you will find business analysts who understand business process design but may not have the required familiarity with the technical aspects. Both make good candidates for project architects.

Whether starting from the business or technical side, project architects need to be shown how to address the full scope of an architecture: the work processes, the architectural pattern, and the mapping of the processes onto the pattern. They must be given the tools and introduced to the methodology. Most importantly, they need to have a mentor—someone they can call when it may not be obvious what to do in a particular situation. This training and mentoring are important facets of the enterprise architect's role.

The Importance of Vision

The importance of communicating vision should not be underestimated. Consider the following thought experiment. You are planning a picnic for your team and their families. To avoid overburdening anyone, you decide to split up the responsibilities, asking one person to select the beverages, another to choose the food, and a third to determine the location for the picnic. Given these assignments, the three people make the incompatible choices shown in Figure 5-6.

What is missing from this exercise is a shared vision of the end result—in this case, the picnic. Imagine now the outcome would be different if the image of Figure 5-7 were presented first. Here you see the vision of the intended event, including the type of food, the type of beverage, and the setting.

Person A: Choose the beverages
- Selects fine wines

Person B: Choose the food
- Decides on a barbeque

Person C: Choose the location
- Chooses a site up a mountain on a hiking trail

These choices are incompatible!

Figure 5-6: *Planning a Picnic without Vision*

Figure 5-7: *A Vision for the Picnic*

Architecture is as much about vision as it is about good design. The project architect defines the vision for the project and the enterprise architect the vision for the enterprise as a whole. It is not sufficient for these architects to have their visions in their heads. They must be effectively shared or the rest of the participants in the process will not be able to make decisions with confidence that they are contributing positively to the realization of the vision.

Summary

The job of an architect is high-level design (i.e., architecture), whether it be of an individual project's efforts or an entire enterprise. These designs characterize the manner in which the enterprise performs its functions (the business processes), the structure and organization of the systems that support these business processes (the architecture pattern), and the mapping of the business processes onto the architecture pattern.

Almost by definition, the work of an architect spans multiple systems and organizations. As such, the architect is effectively determining the changes that are required to those systems and organizations in order to realize the project goals. Doing this job effectively requires a clear understanding of the project charter: the quantified expectations of the project's results, the project's cost and schedule constraints, and the business impact of business processes that fail to execute properly. The architect can significantly reduce integration time by defining an efficient order of assembly for the project components and then overseeing the actual integration test step.

The work of the architect is best accomplished by leading the design effort, not critiquing the designs of others. An analysis of data from real projects shows that this type of leadership can reduce the duration of complex projects by up to 25%—a figure that business and IT ought to find hard to ignore.

Enterprise architectures are not built all at once. Instead, they are realized, piece by piece, through a series of projects. This gives rise to two coordinated architecture roles: the project architect and the enterprise architect. The role of the project architect is to rationalize the changes to business processes and systems within the scope of the current project. The role of the enterprise architect is to define the overall architecture vision and then coordinate the work of the individual projects to contribute to realizing that vision.

Reference architectures play a key role in this dialog between project and enterprise architects. They provide an efficient and effective mechanism for the enterprise architect to document how specific patterns of work ought to be carried out in the intended architecture. When project architects recognize those work patterns, they apply the appropriate reference architectures. This saves time and ensures that the project work is done in a manner consistent with the enterprise architecture vision.

It is important that the architecture vision be shared widely both at the project and enterprise level. This allows business stakeholders to validate the appropriateness of the proposed architecture. It also helps technical stakeholders to understand the origins of the requirements for their components and how those components are expected to participate in the larger design.

Chapter 6

SCA Concepts and Notation

The service-component architecture (SCA) provides a programming model for building applications and systems based on a Service Oriented Architecture (SOA). It provides a model both for the composition of services and for the creation of service components, including the reuse of existing application function within SCA compositions. The SCA specifications can be found on the OSOA Web site,[1] and Marino and Rowley's *Understanding SCA (Service Component Architecture)*[2] provides an excellent overview.

The TIBCO ActiveMatrix™ suite of products is based heavily upon SCA concepts and uses the graphical notation for SCA as one of its design interfaces. Consequently, a basic understanding of SCA concepts and notation is essential to effectively work with TIBCO products. The purpose of this chapter is to provide that overview. However, the chapter is not intended to be comprehensive in this respect.

Despite its name, the service-component architecture does not define complete architectures in the sense that we have been discussing. It only provides the mechanisms for defining architecture patterns that are based on service-oriented architecture principles. For this

---

1. www.osoa.org/display/Main/Service+Component+Architecture+Home

2. Jim Marino and Michael Rowley, *Understanding SCA (Service Component Architecture)*, Boston: Addison-Wesley (2010).

reason, a variety of Unified Modeling Language (UML) notations will be used to provide a more comprehensive view of the architectures and reference architectures as they are discussed.

In this chapter we will examine four major SCA concepts: components, services, references, and composites. We will see how these elements can be wired together to form larger design components and, ultimately, complete solutions.

An Example Service Design

To illustrate the use of SCA concepts and notation we will use the simple architecture pattern shown in Figure 6-1. This pattern shows a service for managing an account balance that, internally, uses a second data management service to actually store and retrieve values. The account balance management is intended to support simple Internet banking.

Looking at the pattern more closely, it involves three components and two service interfaces. The components are the `Consumer-AccountApplication`, the `AccountBalanceManager`, and the

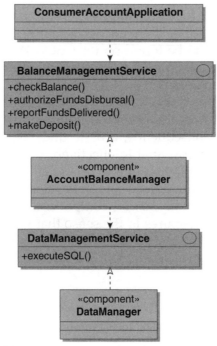

Figure 6-1: *Account Management Example*

DataManager. The services are the `BalanceManagementService` and the `DataManagementService`.

The focus of the following discussion will be the `Account-BalanceManager` component, which implements the functionality of the `BalanceManagementService`. The `AccountBalanceManager`, in turn, uses the functionality of the `DataManager` through the facilities of the `DataManagementService`.

Components and Composites

The basic unit of functional implementation in SCA is the *component*. Figure 6-2 shows the `AccountBalanceManager` being implemented as an SCA component. This component is contained within an SCA *composite*, which is the basic unit of assembly (and deployment) in SCA. Note that while this example is technically correct, from a practical perspective it is not particularly useful since it has no interface for accessing the `AccountBalanceManager` functionality.

A key aspect of SCA is that it allows designs to be assembled from components of various types. Consistent with this philosophy, TIBCO supports a wide variety of implementation types, including:

- TIBCO ActiveMatrix BusinessWorks™

- The Mediation implementation type in TIBCO ActiveMatrix™ Service Bus

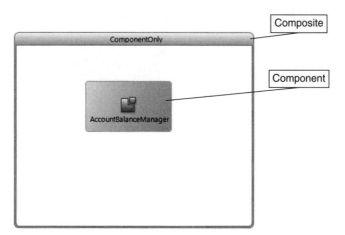

Figure 6-2: *Components and Composites*

- Java
- C++
- Spring
- WebApp
- An SCA composite

In addition to these possibilities, TIBCO Business Studio™ allows components to be created without specifying the implementation type to allow flexibility during the formative stages of designs. Designers can thus sketch an initial design structure and postpone the decision about the actual technology that will be used to implement the functionality.

Services

In order to make the functionality of the `AccountBalanceManager` component accessible, we need to add a *service* to the component (Figure 6-3). In ActiveMatrix Service Bus, a service is an interface (port-Type) defined in a WSDL file. Placing the service icon on the boundary of the component associates the service with the component.

Component services are only accessible to other components within the composite. In order to make the service available outside the composite you need to add a service to the composite and then wire it to the component service (Figure 6-4). A composite service is said to be

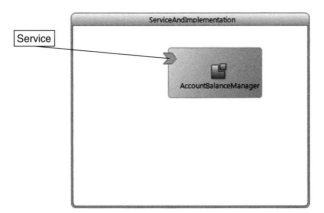

Figure 6-3: *Component with Service*

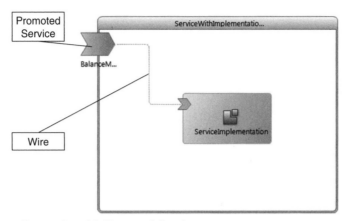

Figure 6-4: *Composite with Promoted Service*

promoted, meaning that it is visible outside the composite, as opposed to the component service that is only visible within the composite. Note that in order to wire the composite service to the component service in ActiveMatrix, both services must be associated with the same WSDL portType.

When a composite with a promoted service is deployed in ActiveMatrix Service Bus, the service becomes bound to an endpoint. This makes it available as a web service and thus accessible to the `ConsumerAccountApplication` or any other external service consumer.

References

In our example, the `AccountBalanceManager` makes use of some functionality provided by the DataManager through the `DataManagementService`. In SCA when a component makes reference to a service, you add an icon indicating the reference to the component (Figure 6-5). In ActiveMatrix Service Bus this reference is associated with the WSDL portType that defines the service interface.

The icon indicates that a reference is being made but does not indicate where the service itself is located. In ActiveMatrix Service Bus it is an error to have a component reference without wiring it to something—hence the error indication in the figure. One way of resolving the reference is to promote the reference as in Figure 6-6. With this

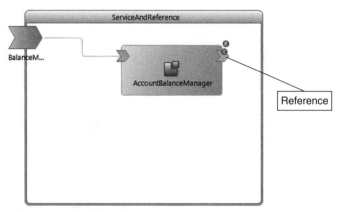

Figure 6-5: *Component with Reference*

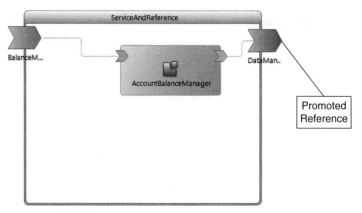

Figure 6-6: *Promoted Reference*

approach, when the composite is either deployed or incorporated into a larger composite, the promoted reference is wired.

Component Type

The services and references associated with a component, together with the component's parameters, define the *component type*. The component type fully defines the component from an external perspective, including the means by which other components can interact with it (the services and references) and the means by which it can be configured (the parameters). Any implementation that conforms to this type specification is an acceptable implementation.

Implementation Type

An implementation type defines the type of technology used to implement a component. SCA allows you to choose from a wide range of implementation types. The implementation types supported in TIBCO ActiveMatrix Service Grid and Service Bus are described in Chapter 9. Be careful not to confuse the component type with the implementation type—they are two different concepts!

Complex Composites

The alternative to using a promoted reference is putting the referenced service and the component providing it into the same composite as the reference and wiring the two together (Figure 6-7).

Composites can also be used as components in other composites. Figure 6-8 shows the full example as a single composite comprised of two other composites: one containing the `ConsumerAccount-Application` and the other containing the `BalanceManager` and `DataManager`.

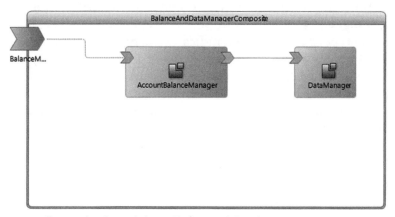

Figure 6-7: *Composite Containing a Referenced Service*

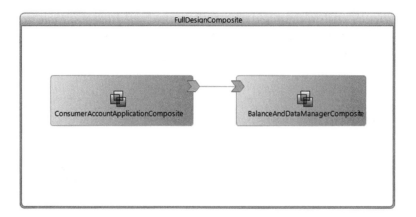

Figure 6-8: *Composite of Composites*

Summary

The service-component architecture standards establish, among other things, a graphical notation for describing architecture patterns. TIBCO Business Studio, provided as part of the TIBCO ActiveMatrix Service Bus, uses this graphical notation as one of its design interfaces.

SCA defines a design in terms of components, services, references, and composites. Components comprise the functional elements of a design and may be of different types. Services are interfaces exposed by components, and components access external services via references. Each service and reference is characterized by a WSDL portType that defines the service interface. A component's services and references, along with its parameters, define its component type. The implementation type of a component indicates the type of technology chosen to implement the component.

SCA assembles components, services, and references into composites. Within a composite, services and references may be wired together. Services and references may also be promoted to the composite, making them accessible from outside the composite. Composites themselves may be used as components in forming other composites.

Part II

TIBCO Product Architecture

Chapter 7

The TIBCO Product Suite

The TIBCO product suite is very broad and comprehensive (Figure 7-1). As such, it is impossible to cover the entire product suite in any practically sized volume. So where do you start when it comes to TIBCO and architecture?

The answer to this question begins with the realization that most solutions built with TIBCO products are distributed systems. These systems involve many different types of components, only some of which are TIBCO products.

By their very nature, distributed systems require components to interact with one another—to connect, interact, and coordinate. Interaction and coordination provide the conceptual focus for *TIBCO Architecture Fundamentals*. They determine the products and design patterns that will be discussed in this book.

Interaction requires communications, and the two most prevalent communications mechanisms being employed today are the Hypertext Transport Protocol (HTTP) and the Java Messaging Service (JMS). Components using HTTP talk directly to one another over the network, and this protocol is amply documented elsewhere. On the other hand, components using JMS for communications require a messaging server. This book discusses the TIBCO Enterprise Messaging Service (EMS), which provides JMS capabilities and much more besides.

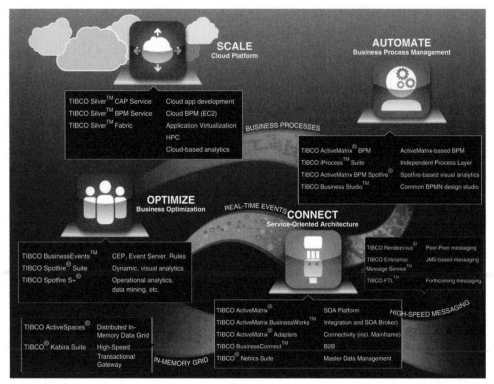

Figure 7-1: *Overview of the TIBCO Product Suite*

Service-oriented architecture (SOA) is an architecture style fol-
lowed in many modern designs. At the core of a modern TIBCO-based
SOA design lie TIBCO ActiveMatrix® Service Bus, TIBCO ActiveMatrix®
Service Grid, and TIBCO ActiveMatrix®BusinessWorks™. Augmenting
these products is a series of TIBCO ActiveMatrix adapters that facilitate
interactions with non-TIBCO components. These products are the primary focus of this book and will be discussed in some detail.

Beyond basic interactions, solutions tend to grow in different directions: composite applications and services, business process management, and business optimization. Each of these areas will be the subject
of a specialized follow-on book addressing that particular area:

- *Architecting Composite Applications and Services with TIBCO*
- *Architecting BPM Solutions with TIBCO*
- *Architecting Complex Event Processing Solutions with TIBCO*

Each of these areas has a core product that is central to most of the solutions built in that area. Composite applications and services are built largely on TIBCO ActiveMatrix Service Bus and Service Grid. In business process management (BPM), solutions are generally built on the TIBCO ActiveMatrix® BPM product. In complex event processing, solutions are generally built on TIBCO BusinessEvents™. For completeness, this book provides a brief overview of these latter two products as well. Information on all TIBCO products can be found at www.tibco. com and www.TIBCOmmunity.com.

Chapter 8

TIBCO Enterprise Message Service™

The TIBCO Enterprise Message Service™ (EMS) product plays two important roles in TIBCO-based designs. One is as an application-level messaging transport, and the other is as the internal application-level communications infrastructure underlying the TIBCO ActiveMatrix Service Bus. Consequently, it is important for an architect to have some familiarity with this product.

Most of the required familiarity with EMS can be acquired through the supplied product documentation. The information presented here is intended merely to provide an overview of the product. For further information, the reader should consult the technical documentation supplied with the product.

Enterprise Message Service™ Product Structure

The Enterprise Message Service product comprises a number of components (Figure 8-1). At its heart, the workhorse component is the EMS server, an operating system executable that manages the distribution of messages between clients. This server, depending on configuration, can store messages in transit in either a file or a database. Designs involving EMS often employ multiple EMS servers for fault tolerance or load distribution.

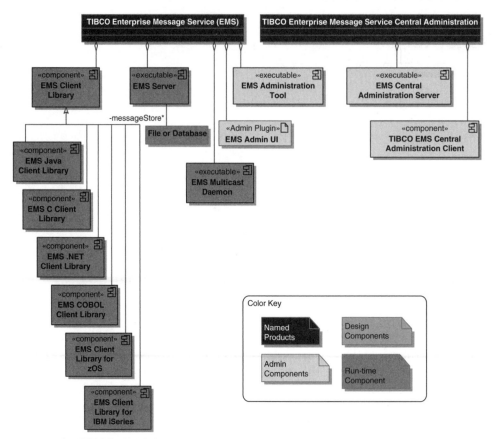

Figure 8-1: *TIBCO EMS Components*

The EMS server is implemented in the C programming language for efficiency. It is important to note that the bulk of the work being performed in the EMS server occurs in two threads, one handling the network I/O and the other interacting with the files or databases used for message persistence. Since the bulk of the work occurs in these two threads, a single EMS server instance will consume little more than two CPU cores when fully loaded.

Companion to the EMS server component are the EMS client libraries provided for the Java, C, C#, .NET, and COBOL programming languages. These libraries provide the facilities for interacting with the EMS server and are incorporated into clients who wish to send and receive messages. The API provided by the EMS Java client library conforms to the Java Messaging Service (JMS) 1.1 specification.[1]

With respect to administration, there are a number of possible approaches. The server itself provides administrative APIs that are accessible from both the Java and .NET client libraries. This makes it possible for applications to administer the server directly. This, in fact, is how TIBCO ActiveMatrix Service Bus manages the underlying EMS server that it uses.

EMS also provides a stand-alone EMS administration tool that provides a command-line administrative interface. Some versions of the TIBCO Administrator™ also provide plugins for EMS administration.

Finally, for those situations in which there are a significant number of EMS servers in use, there is the TIBCO Enterprise Message Service™ Central Administration server. This provides a centralized mechanism for conveniently managing multiple EMS server instances.

Message Delivery Transports

Conventional Message Delivery

In conventional JMS message delivery (Figure 8-2) each exchange between a receiving application and a JMS server involves an individual TCP protocol interaction. Thus the publication of a message to a topic with three subscribers will result in four messages on the network: the original message being sent and an additional message for each of the recipients. It will also require the JMS server to send three outbound messages.

High-Fanout Message Delivery

Some solutions require the delivery of the same message to many recipients. The solution typically involves a JMS Topic with many subscribers. This is typically referred to as a high-fanout situation. When there are a large number of messages being delivered with high fanout, the volume of traffic may be limited by the available network bandwidth. In some cases, the capacity of the JMS server to deliver the messages may also limit the rate at which the messages can be delivered.

---

1. www.oracle.com/technetwork/java/jms/index.html

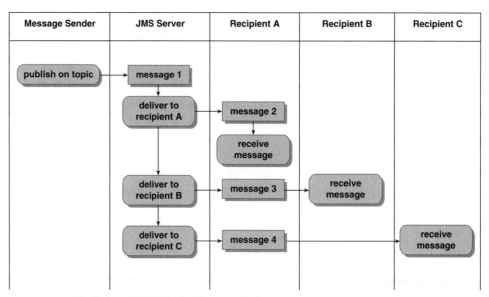

Figure 8-2: *Traditional JMS Topic Message Delivery*

Multicast Message Delivery

To deal with high-fanout situations, EMS provides an alternative message delivery approach that utilizes multicast delivery over the network. Taking advantage of this approach requires a particular style of deployment shown in Figure 8-3. In this deployment pattern each recipient application has an EMS multicast daemon running on the same machine. Communication between the EMS server and the multicast daemon uses multicast and each message appears only once on the network. Communication between the daemon and applications on the same machine use TCP, but with local loopback. These communications do not appear on the network. There are also configuration requirements which are described in the EMS product manuals.

When multicast message delivery is properly configured and deployed, messages are delivered as shown in Figure 8-4. This delivery approach provides two efficiencies: One is that the EMS server only sends each message exactly once regardless of how many recipients there are. This reduces the amount of work the EMS server needs to do for each message. The other is that each message appears exactly once on the network regardless of how many recipients there are. This reduces the required network bandwidth.

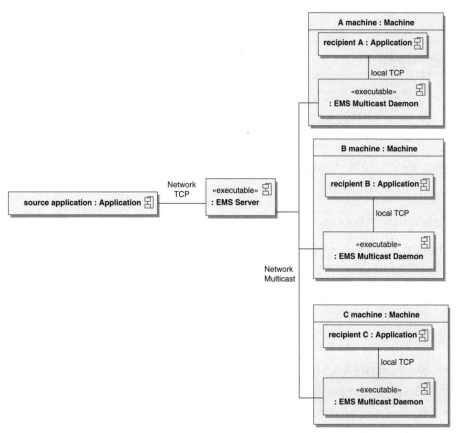

Figure 8-3: *Architecture Pattern for Using Multicast Message Delivery*

There is one important limitation to consider when using this delivery pattern. In traditional JMS message delivery each client explicitly acknowledges the receipt of each message. Thus the JMS server knows whether or not the message was delivered successfully and, in the event of a failed delivery, will attempt to redeliver the message the next time a connection is established with the receiving application. With multicast delivery this acknowledgment is turned off. Consequently, a network issue can cause a loss of messages.

Another consideration with multicast is that the network itself must be multicast-enabled. Furthermore, if the receiving applications and the EMS server are on different subnets, multicast routing between these subnets must be configured. Thus it is administratively more complex to set up multicast routing as opposed to conventional message delivery.

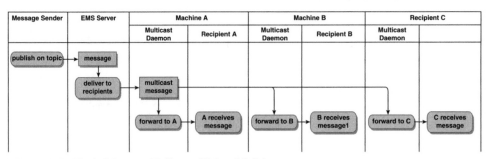

Figure 8-4: *Topic Message Delivery Using Multicast*

Enterprise Message Service Feature Highlights

There are a number of EMS features of architectural interest. These are described in detail in the product manual, but we highlight them here for convenience. They include:

- Multiple message storage options, including both files and databases
- Support of JACI for authorization
- Support of JAAS for custom authentication and authorization
- Message compression
- Bi-directional connectivity with TIBCO Rendezvous® and TIBCO SmartSockets®

Chapter 9

TIBCO ActiveMatrix®

The TIBCO ActiveMatrix Product Suite

The TIBCO ActiveMatrix® (AMX) product suite is a family of related products (Figure 9-1). This chapter provides an overview of these products and their architecture.

The cornerstone of the suite is the TIBCO ActiveMatrix® Service Bus, which provides the foundational infrastructure for building solutions based on the service-component architecture (SCA) concept. TIBCO ActiveMatrix® Service Grid builds on this foundation, adding a number of implementation types that can be used for implementing components. TIBCO ActiveMatrix® BPM adds support for business process management, built on this same framework.

TIBCO ActiveMatrix BusinessWorks™ is an integration and service engine with a graphical programming interface that can be deployed either stand-alone or within the ActiveMatrix Service Bus. The TIBCO ActiveMatrix adapters provide lightweight interfaces to many types of external systems. All adapters can be deployed stand-alone, and some can be deployed within the ActiveMatrix Service Bus.

TIBCO ActiveMatrix® Lifecycle Governance Framework provides lifecycle management, repository, and registry capabilities to the enterprise. Since its operation is relatively independent of the rest of the ActiveMatrix product suite and its manuals provide a good overview of its usage, we will not discuss this product further in this book.

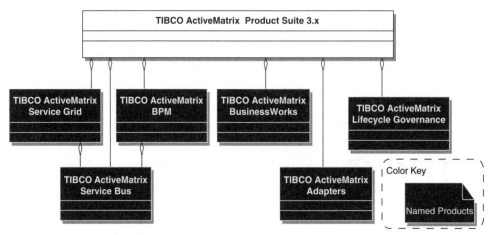

Figure 9-1: *The ActiveMatrix Product Suite*

Basic TIBCO ActiveMatrix Architecture Patterns

The basic architecture pattern for ActiveMatrix deployments is shown in Figure 9-2. Components deployed within ActiveMatrix run in nodes, whose architecture will be examined in a moment. ActiveMatrix components interact with external components via external interfaces and, when deployed on different nodes, interact with each other via a private TIBCO Enterprise Message Service (EMS) instance.

The internal structure of an ActiveMatrix node is shown in Figure 9-3. Components implement application functionality, while bindings provide the service and reference interfaces for these components. Interactions between components and bindings occur via the ActiveMatrix Virtualization Infrastructure that enables communications both within and between nodes. Bindings, in turn, rely on ActiveMatrix Shared Resources such as HTTP clients and servers for the realization of external communication interfaces.

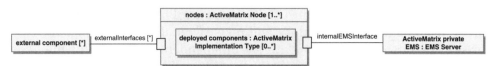

Figure 9-2: *Simplified ActiveMatrix Architecture Pattern*

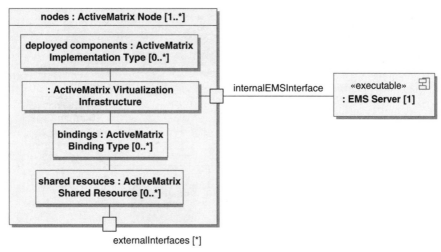

Figure 9-3: *ActiveMatrix Node Internal Structure*

Implementation Types

A component is the basic unit of functionality in ActiveMatrix. ActiveMatrix offers a wide variety of technology choices (implementation types) for implementing components. Figure 9-4 presents an overview of the available implementation types as of the publication of this book.

One of the simplest implementation types is Mediation. It is intended to serve as an intermediary between service providers and service consumers. For this purpose it provides simple and efficient content transformation, augmentation, and routing capabilities and has a simple graphical design interface that does not require coding. The Mediation implementation type is provided as part of the TIBCO ActiveMatrix Service Bus and its use is described in Chapter 14.

The Java and C++ implementation types provide the ability to implement functionality in their respective programming languages. The Spring implementation type enables functionality to be defined using the Spring framework. The WebApp implementation type enables the implementation of web applications with their own HTTP interfaces. These four implementation types are provided as part of the TIBCO ActiveMatrix Service Grid product.

TIBCO ActiveMatrix BusinessWorks provides the ability to implement composite applications and services using a graphical design interface

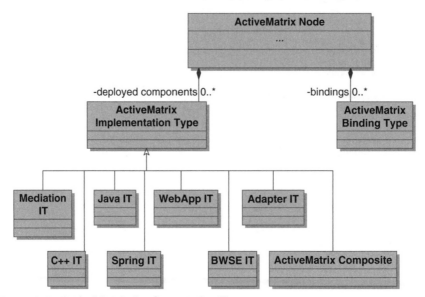

Figure 9-4: *ActiveMatrix Implementation Types*

rather than coding. Its implementations can be deployed either within a stand-alone engine or within the TIBCO BusinessWorks™ Service Engine (BWSE) implementation type in an ActiveMatrix node. The BWSE implementation type is provided as part of the TIBCO Active-Matrix BusinessWorks product.

TIBCO adapters provide lightweight mechanisms for interacting with external systems that can be easily configured through graphical design interfaces. Like BusinessWorks, adapter designs can be deployed as stand-alone adapter engines, and many of them can also be deployed within adapter implementation types in ActiveMatrix nodes. For TIBCO adapters that are deployable in ActiveMatrix, the required implementation type is included with the adapter product. The use of adapters is described in Chapter 15.

The last implementation type is the ActiveMatrix composite. A composite is an SCA construct that has services and references just like any other component (see Chapter 6). Its internal structure, however, comprises one or more components of any type, wired together. Any ActiveMatrix composite can be used as a component within another composite.

Binding Types

Bindings associate transports and protocols with component services and references. ActiveMatrix Service Bus provides a number of binding types (Figure 9-5). The SOAP protocol is supported with binding types for three different transports: HTTP, JMS, and the built-in ActiveMatrix Virtualization infrastructure. Note that the Virtualization binding only provides transport between components deployed within ActiveMatrix nodes.

The JMS binding type enables XML data structures to be sent and received over JMS transports. The EJB binding type enables interactions with enterprise java beans (EJBs) deployed in other environments. The Adapter binding type enables communication with TIBCO adapters. All binding types are provided with the TIBCO ActiveMatrix Service Bus product.

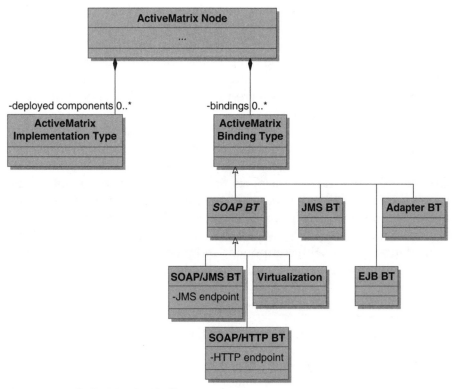

Figure 9-5: *ActiveMatrix Binding Type*

ActiveMatrix Node

The container into which ActiveMatrix composite assemblies are deployed is the node. The default node supplied with ActiveMatrix is a stand-alone executable built on a Java virtual machine (JVM). However, the node is architected in such a way that it, itself, could be deployed within another environment such as an application server. The current product literature should be consulted for an up-to-date list of node deployment options.

Nodes can contain components, bindings, and resources. When a component is deployed to a node it is deployed as an OSGi plugin that is installed into the node. The same is true for bindings and resources.

In order to keep the node lightweight, plugins are not installed into the node until a component (or binding or resource) is deployed to the node. At that time, the ActiveMatrix administrator automatically installs the needed plugins.

As you might imagine, the number of component, binding, and resource types yield many possible configurations for an ActiveMatrix node. Figure 9-6 illustrates a node with most of the possible plugins deployed in it. Although is it unlikely that you would have all of these elements deployed in one node in production, it does illustrate the possibilities. In fact, you might actually find this configuration in a development environment if you were playing with all of the component, binding, and resource types.

Every ActiveMatrix node contains an element known as the policy agent. The policy agent serves as the control point for all policies that are enforced within the node. Policies (which will be discussed in Chapter 13) govern many aspects of node behavior, but some of the more common are access control policies governing authentication, authorization, and encryption. Illustrated in the diagram are the policy enforcement points (PEPs) where these policies can be enforced. Note that all interactions with component and binding types and most interactions with resources can be governed with policies.

TIBCO ActiveMatrix Service Bus

The foundational product in the ActiveMatrix product suite is the Service Bus (Figure 9-7). The major elements of this product are the

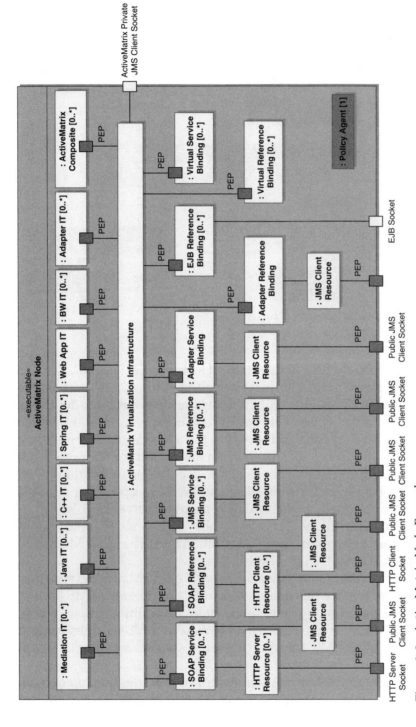

Figure 9-6: *ActiveMatrix Node Example*

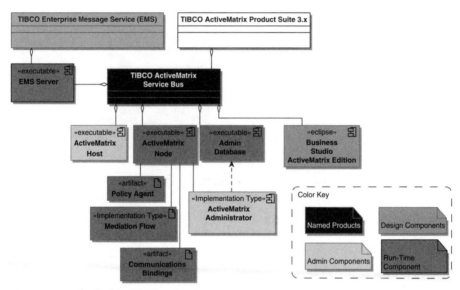

Figure 9-7: *ActiveMatrix Service Bus*

ActiveMatrix Node, the ActiveMatrix Host, the EMS server, and the TIBCO Business Studio™ ActiveMatrix SOA Edition. The node is the container into which components, bindings, and resources are deployed. The ActiveMatrix Host is installed on every machine to which ActiveMatrix is deployed and serves as the administrative representative for ActiveMatrix on that machine. In the default configuration both the node and the ActiveMatrix Host are stand-alone executables, with each node being a Java Virtual Machine (JVM). In upcoming releases, both may be optionally installable in application servers.

Included with the node are the policy agent, all communication bindings, and the Mediation implementation type. The use of Mediation is described in Chapter 14.

While an EMS Server is installed with ActiveMatrix Service Bus, the license for Service Bus does not include a stand-alone EMS license. The EMS Server is only licensed for internal communications within the ActiveMatrix Service Bus. Any other use of EMS (such as using it for a SOAP over JMS transport) requires a separate explicit EMS license.

The TIBCO ActiveMatrix® Administrator provides the deployment and run-time management for ActiveMatrix environments. From a run-time perspective, the administrator is actually an ActiveMatrix component that runs in a dedicated ActiveMatrix node. The administrator's user interface is provided through a web browser interacting directly with the administrator. An associated database is used as a staging location for deployment and configuration information. ActiveMatrix Service Bus includes a HyperSQL database that can be used for this purpose, but its use is only recommended for development environments. Test and production environments should use a production database such as Oracle or Microsoft SQLServer.

TIBCO Business Studio ActiveMatrix SOA Edition provides the development environment for ActiveMatrix. Business Studio is based on Eclipse and uses the service-component architecture (SCA) graphical notation to specify ActiveMatrix designs.

TIBCO ActiveMatrix Service Grid

The TIBCO ActiveMatrix Service Grid product is built upon ActiveMatrix Service Bus and includes all the elements of Service Bus (Figure 9-8). Service Grid simply adds four implementation types: Java, C++, WebApp, and Spring. The Java implementation type makes it possible to create Java implementations of components that execute within an ActiveMatrix node, which is a Java run-time environment. The C++ implementation type makes it possible for components written in C++ to be accessed from within the Java-based ActiveMatrix node. The C++ code itself runs in a separate process. The Spring[1] implementation types allow Java code with the Spring extensions to run within the ActiveMatrix node. The WebApp implementation type allows web applications consisting of JavaServer Pages (JSP) and Java servlets to be run within the ActiveMatrix node. The WebApp implementation type exposes an HTTP (or HTTPS) interface with which browsers can interact. For more details on these implementation types, please consult the product manuals.

---

1. For an overview of Spring, see Craig Walls, *Spring in Action, Second Edition*, Greenwich, CT: Manning Publications (2008).

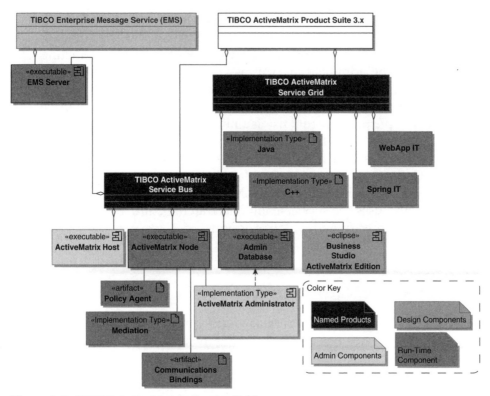

Figure 9-8: *TIBCO ActiveMatrix Service Grid*

ActiveMatrix Environments and Administration

Perspectives on Run-Time Environments

There are two common ways to think about organizing and managing the elements when it comes to deployment: logical and physical. The logical approach groups elements that are somehow related. This kind of grouping typically includes elements that are already deployed (from other projects) as well as the elements presently being deployed.

The physical approach groups elements by the specific physical environment in which they are running. Traditionally the environment has been a physical machine, but technology evolution has added virtual machines and potentially individual application server instances as alternatives.

IT shops require both kinds of grouping. Logical grouping lets you manage things from a functional perspective, while physical grouping helps you manage physical environments. For this reason, TIBCO ActiveMatrix supports both of these approaches.

Logical Environments

ActiveMatrix solutions are deployed into nodes. In a typical solution life cycle, the same design may be deployed into a number of different environments: development, test, production, and so on. To support this, ActiveMatrix provides the notion of an environment, which is simply a logical grouping of nodes (Figure 9-9). Each node belongs to exactly one ActiveMatrix environment. For the most part, when you see the term *environment* in ActiveMatrix documentation, it is this logical grouping that is being discussed.

Physical Environments

AMX nodes, of course, need to reside in some physical environment as well. Figure 9-10 shows how physical environments are organized in ActiveMatrix. A physical environment contains one or more ActiveMatrix hosts, each of which has a number of nodes associated with it. The host is an administrative entity that manages its associated nodes and all the related files in that physical environment. In the TIBCO documentation, the term *instance* refers to a physical environment.

In the base product configuration, a physical environment is simply an operating system instance, and hosts and nodes are stand-alone executables running under the operating system. The stand-alone nodes are individual java runtime environments (JREs). However, the

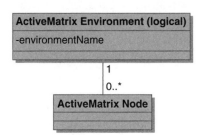

Figure 9-9: *ActiveMatrix Logical Environment Structure*

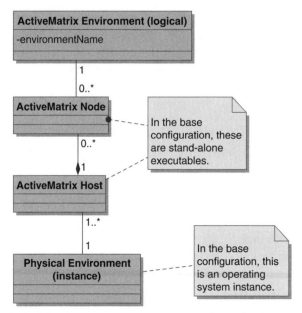

Figure 9-10: *ActiveMatrix Execution Environment Organization*

product is architected in such a way that future releases may be able to support physical environments like application server instances. In such environments the host and its associated nodes will be logical entities within the application server rather than stand-alone executables. From a terminology perspective, in the ActiveMatrix product documentation the physical environment is commonly referred to as an *instance.*

Each node belongs to exactly one logical environment and exactly one physical environment. A single ActiveMatrix logical environment can have nodes in multiple physical environments. Nodes on multiple machines can be part of a single logical environment. Conversely, nodes belonging to multiple logical environments can be present in the same physical environment. If you have separate logical environments for development and test, you can have both development and test nodes on the same machine.

Administration Organization

Administrative tasks are managed by the TIBCO ActiveMatrix Administrator (Figure 9-11). The administrator is itself, an ActiveMatrix

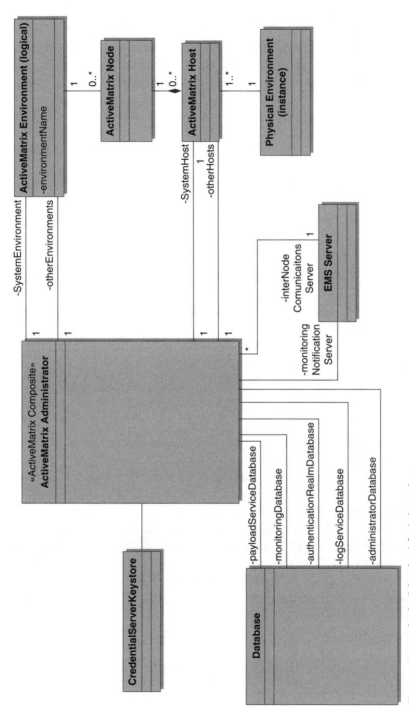

Figure 9-11: *ActiveMatrix Administration*

85

composite running in its own logical environment. This logical environment is called the System Environment and contains a single node called the System Node on which the administrator is deployed. This node runs in a physical environment, and the host in that environment is called the System Host. Note that this physical environment, particularly in development, may contain other nodes belonging to other logical environments as well.

Each host is associated with a single administrator. All administrative activity in a physical environment is carried out by the host associated with the administrator. This includes the creation, configuration, removal, starting, and stopping of the nodes belonging to that host (more on this later).

The administrator uses a number of supporting components: a credential server keystore, one or more databases, and one or two EMS servers. As indicated in the diagram, there are five different roles that can be played by the database. The actual database playing each role is specified individually so that anywhere from one to five databases can be used. Similarly, the EMS servers play two distinct roles, which can be played by either a common server or separate EMS servers.

ActiveMatrix File System Folder Structures

From time to time you may need to know where ActiveMatrix stores information in the file system. This section provides a quick overview.

There are two folder structures created by ActiveMatrix. One is the *installation folder* created when you install the product. All files created during the installation process are placed in this folder. You typically need only one installation folder, regardless of the number of machines on which ActiveMatrix will eventually run. On Windows, the default location is `C:\Program Files\tibco`.

The other folder is the *configuration folder*. Its location is specified when you run the TIBCO Configuration Tool (TCT) at the end of the installation process. This tool is used to create the ActiveMatrix Hosts and the System Node with its Administrator. The tool can place these components in any physical environment, and all files created during configuration are placed in this folder in that physical environment. The default location for the configuration folder is under `C:\Program Data\amx-3`.

Figure 9-12 shows the configuration folder sub-structure. The region under `amx-3/data/admin` is divided into three sections. The

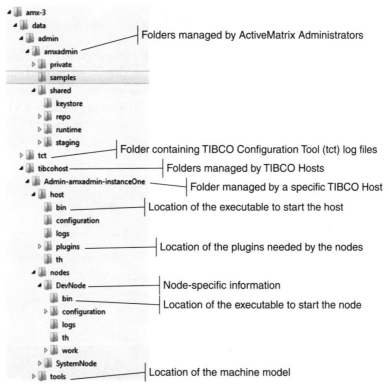

Figure 9-12: *Configuration Folder Structure*

first, `amxadmin`, contains all of the information actually managed by the administrator. The second, `tct`, contains all of the log files created by the TIBCO Configuration Tool. If you have any problems during the configuration process, this is the first place to look. The third, `tibcohost`, contains all of the information being managed by the TIBCO Hosts. In it you will find a sub-folder for each TIBCO Host that has been defined.

In the folder for a specific TIBCO host you will find three sub-folders: The `host` folder contains the executable for starting the host, the host's configuration, and all of the plugins needed by the nodes being managed by the host. The `nodes` folder contains a sub-folder for each node managed by the host. Finally, the `tools` folder contains the machine model, which defines the configuration of the host and all the nodes.

ActiveMatrix Solution Life Cycle

The architecture pattern for AMX administrative activities is shown in Figure 9-13. Solution designs are created in Business Studio and are exchanged with the administrator via the file system. The administrator directs hosts to take action by sending JMX[2] commands, and if the command requires access to a file, that file is retrieved via HTTP. Thus the interactions between the administrator and host are independent of the file system.

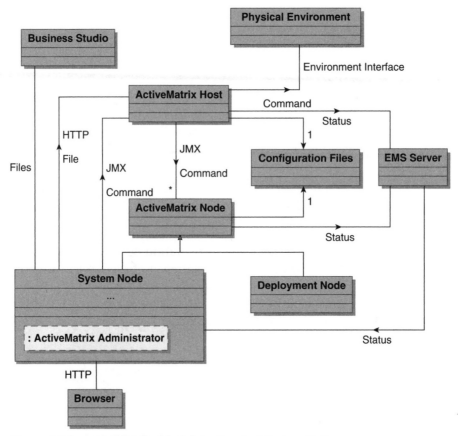

Figure 9-13: *ActiveMatrix Administrative Architecture Pattern*

2. http://java.sun.com/javase/technologies/core/mntr-mgmt/javamanagement/

The host takes action in several ways. It can interact with nodes via JMX commands, interact with the execution environment via its interface (e.g., command line), and interact with configuration files in the local file system. Status updates are sent to the administrator via the EMS monitoring and notification server. Nodes can read configuration files from the execution environment file system and send status updates to the administrator via the EMS monitoring and notification server.

An important element in the execution environment is the machine model (Figure 9-14). There is one machine model per host in each environment. The machine model is a file that contains the configuration definition for all of the nodes in the environment being managed by the host. When a node starts up or is commanded by the host, it reads the machine model to get its configuration. Much of this configuration is a list of the OSGI plugins (and features) that comprise the node. After reading the configuration, the node loads the required plugins and features.

Figure 9-15 shows the ActiveMatrix solution life cycle from design through deployment. An ActiveMatrix solution is created in Business Studio and exported in the form of a distributed application archive (DAA) that contains an application template and is stored in the file system. The application template contains a root composite and a set of related configuration files, including nested composites, WSDL files, substitution variable files, and resource templates.

From the administrator, the target logical environment for the solution is selected (or created, if necessary) and the DAA is imported. From

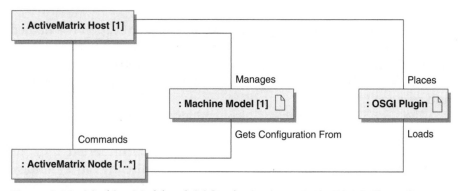

Figure 9-14: *Machine Model and OSGI Plugins in an ActiveMatrix Execution Environment*

Figure 9-15: *ActiveMatrix Solution Life-Cycle Process*

this, the application is created and named. This application is a named copy of the root composite along with its substitution variables. The reason for this copy process is that it allows multiple instances of the same design (DAA) to be independently named, configured, deployed, and managed.

The imported DAA may also contain templates for resources required by the application (things like HTTP servers and clients, JMS clients, etc.). These templates, if needed, can be imported into the administrator. Note that in many cases you will already have identical templates in the administrator. In such cases it is not necessary to import the resource template.

Using the resource templates, the needed resources are created on the nodes to which the solution fragments will be deployed. The administrator accomplishes this by directing the relevant host to place the OSGI plugins and features in the execution environment, updating the node's machine model, and either directing the node to load the required plugin or, in some cases, stopping and starting the node.

Once the resource instances are in place, the application can be deployed by the following sequence of administrator actions:

1. The administrator examines the application to determine if it needs any supporting OSGI plugins (such as the support for a particular implementation type).

2. It determines which fragments of the solution are to be deployed as OSGI plugins on the node.

3. It directs the hosts to position the required OSGI plugins and update the machine models.

4. It tells the hosts to command the affected nodes to re-read the machine model and load the needed plugins.

5. It directs the hosts to start the components.

Part of the deployment may include services that provide SOAP endpoints. Since the details of the endpoint may not be known until the service is actually deployed, after deployment it may be necessary to generate the WSDL containing the endpoint definition.

Deploying SCA Designs on ActiveMatrix Nodes

The ActiveMatrix Business Studio design environment uses SCA notation to specify ActiveMatrix designs. There are, however, many ways in which these designs can be deployed within an ActiveMatrix environment. This section explores, by example, the various deployment options.

Service and Component Deployment

Services (interfaces) and components (implementations) are independently deployable in ActiveMatrix. Figure 9-16 shows a simple design consisting of a single service and its implementation. In this example,

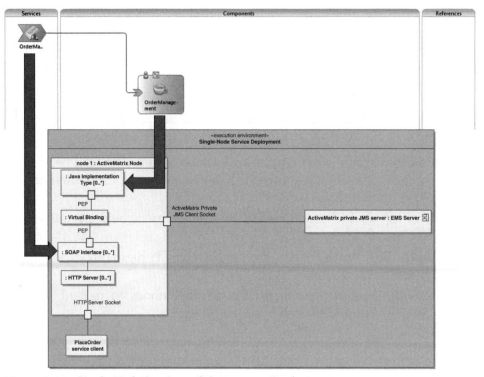

Figure 9-16: *Single-Node Service and Component Deployment*

both are deployed on a single ActiveMatrix node. Communication between them, by default, is fully contained within the node.

An alternate deployment for this design is shown in Figure 9-17. Here the service and component are deployed on different nodes. Communication between them occurs via the ActiveMatrix EMS server. The administration of this server (i.e., the setup of communications between the service and corresponding component) is fully automated. No user action is required, even if the service or the component is moved to a different node.

Service, Component, and Reference Deployment

Like services and components, references are also explicitly deployable. Figure 9-18 shows a simple design consisting of a single service, the component that implements it, and a reference that the component makes. In this example, all three elements are deployed onto a single ActiveMatrix node.

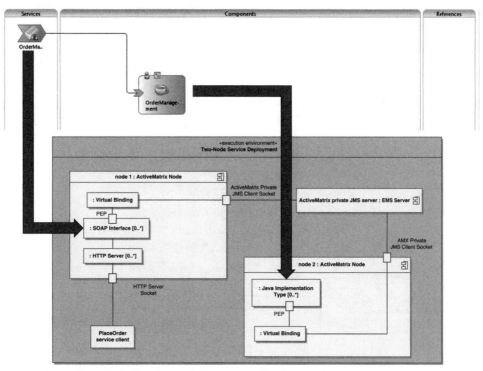

Figure 9-17: *Two-Node Service and Component Deployment*

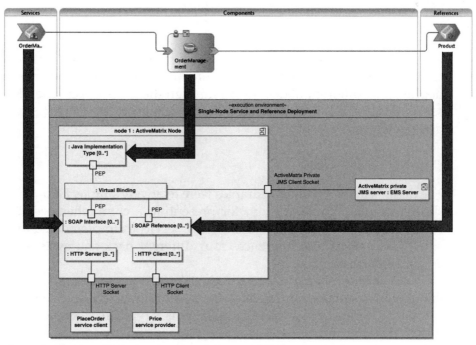

Figure 9-18: *One-Node Service, Component, and Reference Deployment*

93

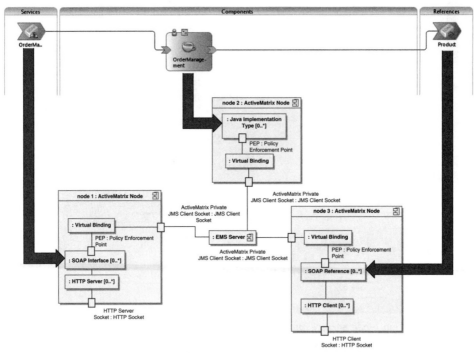

Figure 9-19: *Three-Node Service, Component, and Reference Deployment*

Alternatively, this same design could be deployed to three different nodes (Figure 9-19). Once again, communication among elements deployed on different nodes occurs through the EMS server. The EMS server is automatically configured by the administrator as part of the deployment.

Complex Composite

The designs in the previous examples were relatively simple. Figure 9-20 shows a more complex design for presenting a comprehensive customer view across multiple systems. The service is implemented by a single component that references four different back-end systems to assemble the view.

The simplest deployment for this design is the one shown in Figure 9-21. Here the component, along with the service and all of the references, is deployed on a single node. This is typical of a deployment during development.

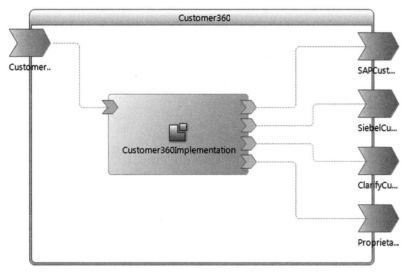

Figure 9-20: *Customer 360 Example Design*

Figure 9-22 shows the same design deployed on four different nodes. Here two instances of the Customer 360 component are deployed, sharing the processing of the Customer 360 Service requests. Both components share the same references to the external systems.

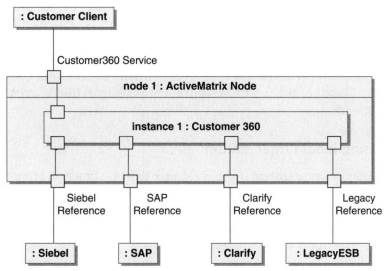

Figure 9-21: *One-Node Customer360 Deployment*

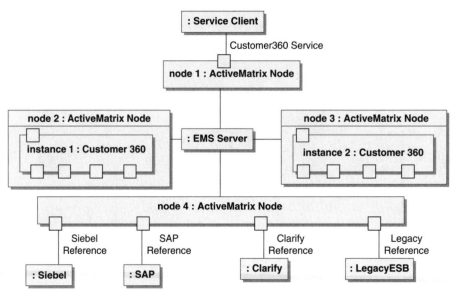

Figure 9-22: *Four-Node Customer360 Deployment*

TIBCO ActiveMatrix BPM

The TIBCO ActiveMatrix BPM product is built on top of the Active-Matrix Service Bus and provides comprehensive support for architecting and implementing BPM solutions. There is much more to architecting these solutions than can be covered in this book, and this will be the subject of the upcoming *Architecting BPM Solutions with TIBCO®*. Here we will confine ourselves to a brief overview of the product and a sketch of what a BPM solution looks like in the ActiveMatrix environment.

BPM Functional Organization

The functional organization of ActiveMatrix BPM is shown in Figure 9-23. The process manager oversees the execution of business processes, including the logic that determines the sequencing of activities and the conditions under which they are performed. The work manager oversees the execution of individual work tasks, including determining who is eligible to work on each task. The work manager can use information in LDAP for this purpose. Both the process manager and work manager provide web service interfaces to access their functionality.

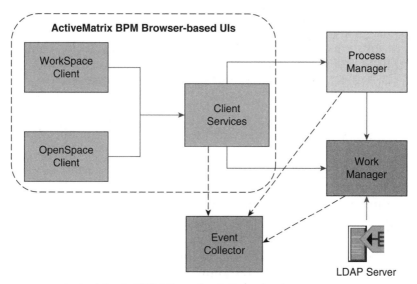

Figure 9-23: *ActiveMatrix BPM Functional Organization*

Two types of browser-based interfaces are provided. The WorkSpace client is a BPM application based on the TIBCO™ General Interface technology. It provides a comprehensive user-configurable browser-based environment for starting business processes and viewing, opening, working on, and completing process tasks. The Openspace client is similar in terms of functionality but is based on the Google Web Toolkit (GWT).[3] Both types of interfaces are extensible. Full custom user interfaces can also be built using the web services interfaces of the process manager and work manager.

The event collector gathers information about all BPM activity including user actions, process status changes, and work item status changes. It provides the raw data necessary to monitor and audit process execution at all levels of detail, ranging from individual events (e.g., a single user action, a single work item completion) to aggregate process statistics (e.g., the average completion time for a process, the peak execution rate for an activity).

3. http://code.google.com/webtoolkit/

BPM Solution Deployment

A BPM solution consists of two major composites: a solution composite and a BPM composite (Figure 9-24). The BPM composite contains the components that come predefined with the ActiveMatrix BPM product. It exposes five public web-service interfaces and a private client services HTTP interface. The public interfaces, described in the product documentation, provide access to the product functionality both for use by BPM solutions and external applications. The proprietary client services provide functional support for the Openspace and Workspace clients provided with the product.

Complementing the BPM composite is the solution composite. It contains all of the solution-specific components defined in the Business Studio design environments. These include process models, organizational models, and customizations to the user interfaces.

As of this writing, both the solution composite and the BPM composite have to be deployed onto a single distinguished ActiveMatrix node. It is anticipated that this constraint will be relaxed in an upcoming release, not only allowing these two composites to be deployed on separate nodes, but also allowing their sub-components to be distributed across multiple nodes. Please consult the product documentation for the latest deployment options. Aside from this constraint, ActiveMatrix BPM solutions are deployed in the same manner as other ActiveMatrix solutions.

Summary

The TIBCO ActiveMatrix product suite comprises a number of products, including the ActiveMatrix Service Bus, ActiveMatrix Service Grid, ActiveMatrix BusinessWorks, ActiveMatrix adapters, ActiveMatrix Lifecycle Governance Framework, and ActiveMatrix BPM.

The ActiveMatrix Service Bus node provides the deployment environment for the suite of products. It can house components, services, references, and resources. When instances on different nodes need to communicate with one another, they do so via an automatically configured TIBCO EMS server in the background. Components can be implemented in a variety of technologies, including Mediation, Java, C++, Spring, and WebApp. Service and reference bindings can be provided

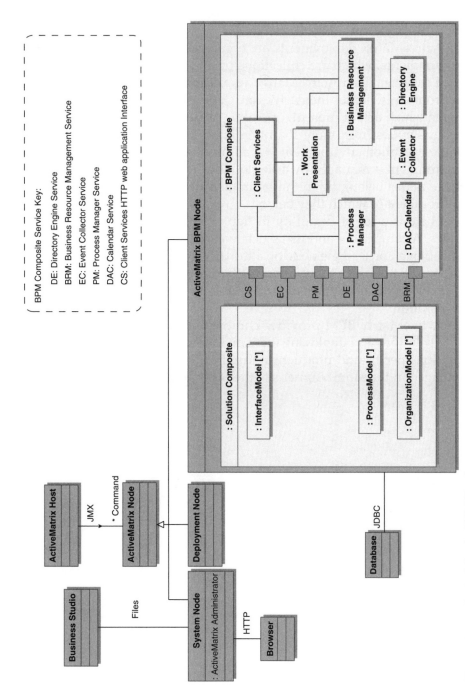

Figure 9-24: *ActiveMatrix BPM Deployment*

99

for SOAP with HTTP, JMS, or virtualization transports, XML over JMS, and EJB interaction.

ActiveMatrix deployments are organized into one or more logical environments, which are collections of nodes that are being administered together. Each ActiveMatrix administrator manages one or more environments. Nodes themselves are deployed into execution environments which are, at present, operating system instances. It is possible to have nodes from more than one logical environment present in a single execution environment. All administrator work in an execution environment is managed by a single TIBCO host. The host manages all of the nodes belonging to that administrator regardless of the logical environment to which they belong.

There is a lot of flexibility in deploying designs on ActiveMatrix nodes. A component and its associated services and references can all be deployed on a single node or, alternatively, each can be deployed on a separate node—without altering the design. This allows for maximum flexibility in support of fault tolerance, high availability, and load distribution.

ActiveMatrix BPM provides comprehensive support for building BPM solutions and deploying them on the ActiveMatrix platform. Both solution-specific and product-standard components are deployed and managed in the same manner as other ActiveMatrix components.

Chapter 10

TIBCO
BusinessEvents™

TIBCO BusinessEvents is a product suite that supports complex event processing. As with BPM, the topic of building solutions requiring complex event processing is beyond the scope of this book and will be the topic of the upcoming book *Architecting Complex Event Processing Solutions with TIBCO*. Here we will provide a conceptual overview of complex event processing and describe the architecture of the TIBCO BusinessEvents product.

Complex Event Processing

Events occur in many places in information systems: A message is sent, a file is created, a user initiates a login. These raw events (or technical events, as they are often called) are things that you can observe. Some of them are meaningful in their own right: A single message might tell you that a package addressed to XYZ Systems has been shipped.

Other events, however, may not be as simple to interpret. Interpretation may require some additional information—some context. The shipment of the package, for example, might mark the completion of an order in the (intentionally oversimplified) process of Figure 10-1. However, to know that the just-shipped package completes the fulfillment of order number 948756 from XYZ Systems, you need more

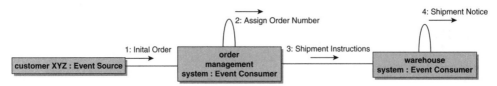

Figure 10-1: *Order Life-Cycle Event Sequence*

information. If, for example, you had captured earlier raw events that marked the placement of the order, the assigning of the order number, the generation of the shipping request to the warehouse, and the assignment of the tracking number to the shipment, you might be able to infer that the shipment marked the completion of the order. Understanding that the final shipment event marks the completion of the order requires understanding the information in these events and correlating them. This event capture, information extraction, and event correlation comprise the world of complex event processing.

Complex event processing is built on a stream of raw events (Figure 10-2). Some of these events are consumed as-is: Their meaning is sufficiently clear to the event consumers that the consumer knows what they represent and can determine what action to take. In other cases, multiple events must be correlated to determine their meaning. In such cases the stream of events is fed to a complex event processor. The processor is configured to analyze the stream of events and recognize particular sequences or patterns that indicate that some business-significant event has occurred: Order 948756 is now complete. A business event is then generated and passed on to the event consumer who will decide what action to take.

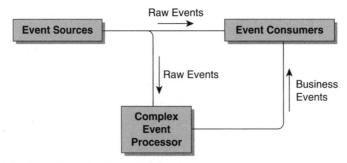

Figure 10-2: *Basic Complex Event Processing*

Information Extraction, Caching, and Persistence

Some situations call for additional processing above and beyond simply recognizing business events. Information from events often needs to be extracted and saved for later use. In the order example you might want to capture and retain the information shown in Table 10-1. With this data you can now correlate the initial order with the shipment instructions and shipment notice to determine whether all the ordered items have been shipped.

TIBCO BusinessEvents provides facilities for modeling the information in events as well as concepts. Concepts are typically abstractions such as orders, shipments, and products. Information about these abstractions is found in individual events, but the abstraction itself provides a location in which this information can be accumulated and maintained. By default, this information is cached in memory and may be distributed across multiple BusinessEvents instances and multiple machines. BusinessEvents provides two optional mechanisms for information persistence.

State Machine Modeling

It is often useful to have a milestone-level model of the process that is supposed to be executing. Figure 10-3 shows a simple order life cycle that indicates which events mark the transitions between order states (milestones). The state machine model simplifies the recording of past history and depicts the allowed courses of action. As each event comes in, the state machine is updated to reflect the current state. Then the state machine provides a convenient context for interpreting the next event.

Table 10-1: *Information Extracted from Order Events*

Event	Extracted Data
Initial order	Ordered items; purchase request number
Assign order number	Purchase request number; order number
Shipment instructions	Items to be shipped; order number; shipment identifier
Shipment notice	Shipment identifier; items actually shipped, date, time

Figure 10-3: *State Model of an Order Life Cycle*

BusinessEvents provides state machine modeling as part of the Data Modeling extension. This includes UML 1.2 modeling of state machines, the ability to associate the state machine with a concept to represent the concept's life cycle, and the ability to model timeouts (the failure to take a transition within a specified period of time).

Event Channels

TIBCO BusinessEvents provides a number of configurable channels for sending and receiving events. These include:

- JMS: Send and receive JMS messages, particularly via the TIBCO Enterprise Message Service.
- HTTP, including SOAP: Send and receive HTTP messages.
- TIBCO Rendezvous®: Send and receive TIBCO Rendezvous messages.
- TCP Channels: Connect to data sources not otherwise available through channels.
- Local: Connect to other agents co-located in the same BusinessEvents engine.

The JMS and HTTP channels can, of course, be used to interact with TIBCO ActiveMatrix components, making their full capabilities available to BusinessEvents.

Rules and Decisions

At the heart of the complex event processor sits a rules engine. Rules have the general form [condition]→[action]. Broadly speaking, the conditions allow you to examine the current event, any previous event in the cache, information in the cache, and the state of state machines. Actions include adding and removing events from the cache; adding, removing, and updating information in the cache; updating the state of state machines; and generating events.

The basic structure of rules, while powerful, is often difficult for nonprogrammers to work with. For this reason, TIBCO BusinessEvents provides the Decision Manager with alternate interfaces for designing rules that are easier for nontechnical personnel to use. It provides a spreadsheet-style format that is familiar to businesspeople, making it easier to write and maintain business rules. The state machine model is another design interface that actually creates rule structures and concept definitions (the states themselves).

Queries

When situations get complex, sometimes it is difficult to represent a situation in terms of rules and state machines. In such cases it may be simpler to query the information in the cache to determine whether a particular condition exists. Typically, these queries are executed in the rule-processing cycle either as part of the rule evaluation or just prior to rule evaluation.

Visualization

Complex event processing deals with a large volume of events and extracts higher-level information. Sometimes this higher-level information is used to initiate interactions with other systems (e.g., by generating business events), but at other times it is a human being who needs to be aware of the situation. This is the purpose of the BusinessEvents Views extension. It provides the ability to define user interfaces (typically tables and graphs) that are animated by BusinessEvents-supplied information. These displays are typically used to show real-time status and provide visual alerts for situations requiring action.

BusinessEvents Solution Roles

Basic Solution Role of a Complex Event Processor

The most basic solution role for a complex event processor is as a generator of business events that, in turn, drive activity in other solution components (Figure 10-4). These business events are essentially announcements that certain business-relevant events have occurred. These events may drive the execution of a business process managed by a BPM engine, invoke specific SOA services, or simply be inputs to other systems that are part of the solution. The key role here is that the complex event processor is interpreting raw events and generating business-meaningful events.

Director Role

The other major role that BusinessEvents can play is that of director (Figure 10-5). In this role BusinessEvents is not only recognizing business events but also deciding what actions to take as a result. These actions can range from simply updating a status visualization through orchestrating a complete business process execution. However, a word of caution is advisable here with respect to business processes: It is not easy to understand a business process that is defined by rules. This approach should be taken only when there are so many variations in the business process that it is not practical to represent the process using BPM or Business Works.

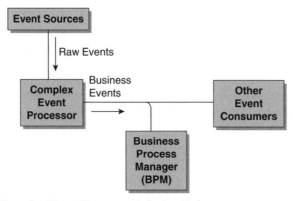

Figure 10-4: *Complex Event Processor Solution Role*

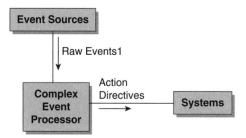

Figure 10-5: *Complex Event Processor Director Role*

TIBCO BusinessEvents Product Suite

The TIBCO BusinessEvents product suite consists of five products (Figure 10-6). The core product is TIBCO BusinessEvents. It provides basic event processing and UML modeling of concepts and events. It has a rules engine and a data grid that allows data to be distributed across multiple engines. It provides an eclipse-based design environment with an integrated debugger and has several monitoring and management options.

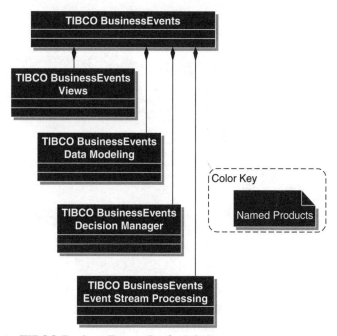

Figure 10-6: *TIBCO BusinessEvents Product Suite*

TIBCO BusinessEvents™ Views

The views extension, which requires the base BusinessEvents product, provides the ability to add real-time displays of objects in Business-Events. These displays make it convenient to visualize levels of activity or processing trends and provide a mechanism for using visual alerts to bring attention to exceptions. Figure 10-7 is an example of a BusinessEvents Views display.

TIBCO BusinessEvents™ Data Modeling

This extension to BusinessEvents adds capabilities in two areas: data modeling and state machine modeling. On the data modeling side, the extension adds the ability to introspect into relational database schema definitions and automatically generate the corresponding Business-Events concepts. It also adds template-based queries and the ability to have transactional interactions with databases.

On the state machine end, the extension adds a visual UML 1.2 state machine modeling tool. The resulting state machines are used to model

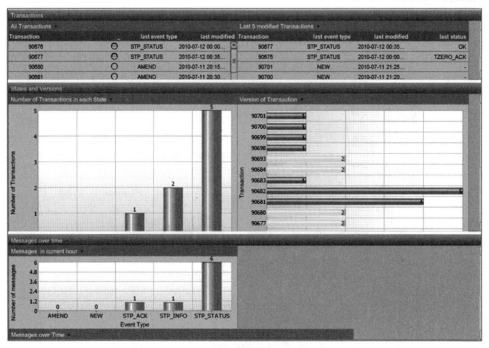

Figure 10-7: *TIBCO BusinessEvents Views Display Example*

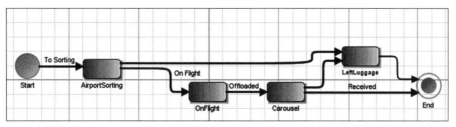

Figure 10-8: *State Model of Airline Luggage Handling*

the life cycle of concepts (e.g., orders). It also adds the ability to model timeouts (the failure to take a transition). This makes it possible to identify events that should have happened, but did not, and take appropriate action.

Figure 10-8 shows a state machine model of the handling of luggage by an airline. This model can then be used to keep track of the state of each individual piece of luggage as it moves through the system.

TIBCO BusinessEvents™ Decision Manager

The Decision Manager extension is designed to make it easier for business users to define business rules. It allows a business user to define, test, and deploy business rules using a spreadsheet-style interface. It provides facilities to import and export rules from actual spreadsheets so that business users can work with spreadsheets directly. The extension can check rules for both completeness and consistency, and can automatically generate test data from rules. Figure 10-9 shows the user interface for the Decision Manager.

TIBCO BusinessEvents™ Event Stream Processing

This extension adds capabilities in two areas: pattern matching and queries. For pattern matching, the extension allows patterns in the event stream to be described in an English-like format, making it easier to define these patterns. It also provides the capability of modeling temporal relationships both between discrete points in time and between intervals. Relationships can be expressed within sliding or tumbling analysis windows. Actions can be initiated for both positive and negative outcomes.

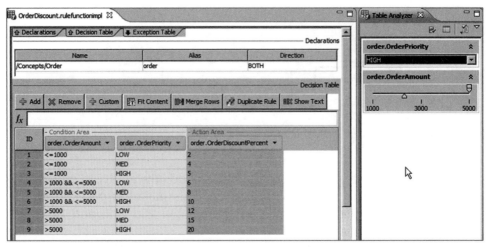

Figure 10-9: *TIBCO BusinessEvents Decision Manager User Interface*

The extension also adds query agent capabilities, placing query objects in the cache engine that allow both continuous and snapshot queries of the cached information. Queries are expressed using the Object Query Language (OQL) from the Object Data Management Group.[1]

BusinessEvents Solution Deployment

BusinessEvents solutions are deployed in one or more BusinessEvents engines that are grouped together into a BusinessEvents cluster (Figure 10-10). The cluster defines a multicast group that is the mechanism by which the engines communicate with one another.

Each engine contains one or more processing units that can be of different types: inference agent, cache agent, dashboard agent, and query agent. The inference agent contains the basic event and rule processing structure. The cache agent manages the event and concept information cache and coordinates the distribution of this information across multiple engines. The dashboard agent manages the visualizations being provided by BusinessEvents. The query agent manages the queries being executed against the cache.

---

1. www.odbms.org/odmg/

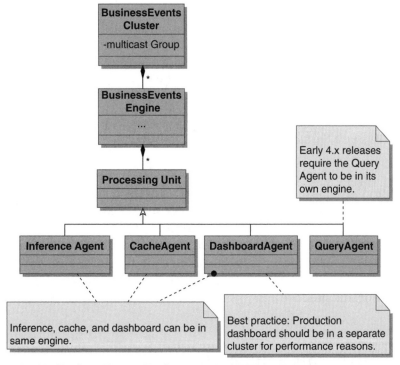

Figure 10-10: *BusinessEvents Deployment Architecture Pattern*

The early releases of BusinessEvents version 4 impose some restrictions on which combinations of agents can be run in a single engine. In particular, these releases require that the query agent be run in its own engine. With this constraint, a minimal deployment of a BusinessEvents solution involving all four agent types would involve two Business-Events engines as shown in Figure 10-11.

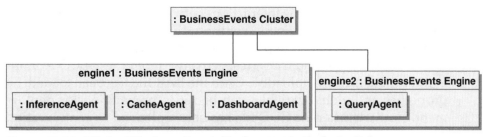

Figure 10-11: *Minimal Business Events Deployment in Early 4.x Releases*

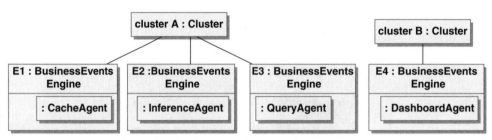

Figure 10-12: *Example Production BusinessEvents Deployment*

Although it is technically possible to run the dashboard agent in the same cluster and engine as the inference and cache agents, it is a best practice to deploy it on its own cluster and engine in production. This is to keep the processing involved in creating the displays from having an adverse impact on the performance of the inference and cache agents. Figure 10-12 shows an example of a production deployment following this practice.

BusinessEvents Solution Life Cycle

A BusinessEvents solution begins its life in the BusinessEvents Studio (Figure 10-13). Here the solution design is created and saved in an EAR file, and the deployment description is captured in a CDD file. These files are then picked up by the TIBCO Administrator. During deployment, the Administrator communicates using TIBCO Rendezvous or EMS with the TIBCO Runtime Agent™ (TRA) on each machine on which a BusinessEvents engine will be deployed. The TRA places the required configuration information on the local machine's file system, executes command lines to start and stop engines, and communicates with the engines to obtain status information.

Figure 10-14 details the interactions between these components during the life cycle. The BusinessEvents Studio is used to both design the application and define its deployment. Each of these activities results in a separate file (EAR and CDD, respectively). From the TIBCO Administrator these files are uploaded. Once the EAR file has been loaded, its properties and global variables can be set in preparation for deployment. Similarly, after the CDD file has been uploaded its configuration

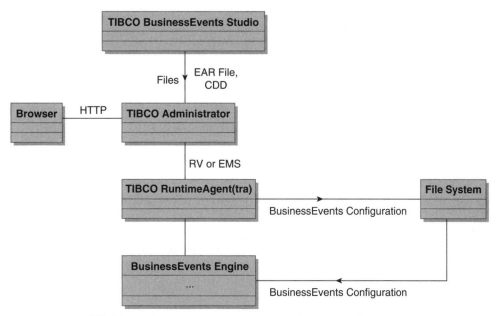

Figure 10-13: *TIBCO BusinessEvents Life Cycle Architecture Pattern*

details can be specified. Upon deployment, the administrator communicates with the TRA on each involved machine to place both configuration files and executables on the machine. When the administrator starts the application, each involved TRA executes the command line for each engine to be started. Upon start-up, each engine reads its configuration files from the local machine and begins processing.

BusinessEvents provides two alternate deployment and management options. One is called BusinessEvents Monitoring and Management. It takes the same inputs (EAR and CDD files) and directly manages the engines in a cluster. It provides the ability to start, stop, and pause individual agents, and to enable and disable rules within an agent. It also provides performance metrics and monitors the health of a BusinessEvents cluster.

The other deployment option is to use scripts. Please consult the product manuals for more details on these options.

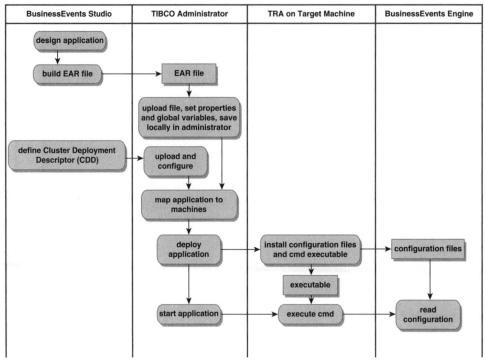

Figure 10-14: *TIBCO BusinessEvents Life Cycle*

Summary

Complex event processing analyzes streams of directly observable events and, using rules, identifies when business-relevant events have occurred. In performing this work, additional capabilities may be required: the extraction and caching of information, the modeling of life cycles using state machines, executing queries against the cached information, and the visualization of status information. All of these capabilities are provided by the BusinessEvents product suite.

BusinessEvents can play two very different roles (or a combination of the two) in a solution. One role is simply that of a business event recognizer: BusinessEvents examines a stream of events and, when it recognizes that a business event has occurred, announces this event to other applications. In this role the other applications decide what to do as a result of that event being recognized.

The other role for BusinessEvents is to determine the appropriate actions to take once a business event has been recognized and then initiate those actions. Some of the actions may be executed by BusinessEvents itself, while in other cases BusinessEvents will make calls to other systems to initiate the actions.

The BusinessEvents product suite consists of the TIBCO Business-Events product and four extension products: TIBCO BusinessEvents Views, TIBCO BusinessEvents Data Modeling, TIBCO BusinessEvents Decision Manager, and TIBCO BusinessEvents Event Stream Processing. BusinessEvents Views adds visualization capability. Business-Events Data Modeling captures database schemas and adds state machine modeling capability. BusinessEvents Decision Manager adds spreadsheet-style interfaces for defining rules. BusinessEvents Event Stream Processing adds query capabilities and the modeling of temporal relationships.

BusinessEvents solutions are deployed on one or more Business-Events engines that are grouped together into clusters. Each engine runs one or more processors, which can be inference agents, cache agents, query agents, and dashboard agents.

BusinessEvents solutions are defined in the BusinessEvents Studio. These designs, and accompanying deployment descriptors, are picked up by the TIBCO Administrator. The Administrator is used to configure the design for deployment and, with the aid of the TIBCO Runtime Agents (TRAs) on the various machines, deploy the design and start the engines. BusinessEvents Monitoring and Management and scripts provide alternative approaches.

Part III

Design Patterns with TIBCO ActiveMatrix®

This portion of the book covers the most common design patterns found in distributed solutions. The patterns are discussed in a progression that begins with the simplest, most common design patterns and builds to more complex, specialized patterns. Each pattern is discussed first in abstract terms and then in terms of its possible TIBCO ActiveMatrix-based implementations.

Chapter 11

Basic Interaction Patterns

This chapter examines the simplest possible interactions between two parties. The architecture pattern for these discussions (Figure 11-1) is, as you would expect, trivial. It consists of the two parties, here referred to as the service consumer and service provider. Despite the fact that we are referring to services, the patterns being discussed can be generalized to represent any interactions between two parties.

The examination of interactions will consider four of the most common ActiveMatrix protocol and transport options: SOAP over HTTP, SOAP over JMS, SOAP over ActiveMatrix Virtualization, and XML over JMS.

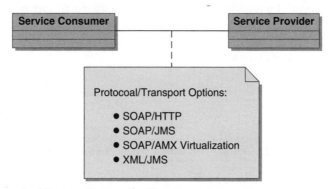

Figure 11-1: *Architecture Pattern for Two-Party Interactions*

Basic Interaction Pattern Overview

There are four basic message exchange patterns between the two parties: In-Only, In-Out, Out-Only, and Out-In. The In-Only pattern is
shown in Figure 11-2. In it, the service consumer sends a single message to the service provider and expects no response. The intent is generally that the arrival of the input will trigger the service provider to do
something useful. Common examples of this pattern include e-mails
and text messages.

   The In-Out pattern (Figure 11-3), also referred to as the request-
reply pattern, is a simple extension of the In-Only pattern that adds a
response (the output) from the service provider. Here the intent is a bit
more explicit: The service consumer provides the input and expects the
arrival of the input to trigger the service provider to do something and
then send a response. This is the pattern you encounter when you execute a search online: You submit the search terms (the input) and expect
a list of "hits" as a response (the output).

   The Out-Only pattern (Figure 11-4) is very similar to the In-Only
pattern, the distinction being that the single message is an output going
from the service provider to the service consumer. Common examples
of this pattern include announcements of various sorts. It is common in
this pattern for there to be many service consumers for a given input
(this will be discussed further in Chapter 12). When the service provider is a system of record for some information, this pattern is suitable
for announcing changes to this information.

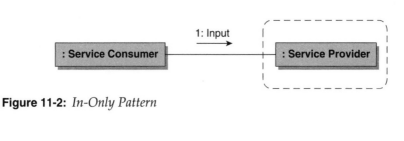

Figure 11-2: *In-Only Pattern*

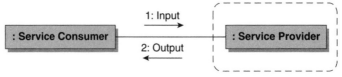

Figure 11-3: *In-Out Pattern*

Figure 11-4: *Out-Only Pattern*

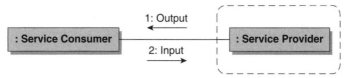

Figure 11-5: *Out-In Pattern*

The Out-In pattern (Figure 11-5) extends the Out-Only pattern to include a response back to the service provider. A common example of this is an automobile recall notice: The manufacturer sends you a notification that there is a defect in your automobile that requires correction. The manufacturer expects a response from you to schedule an appointment and get the defect corrected. Another example is an offer that requires a response.

Example Case Study: A Newspaper

To illustrate these four interaction patterns and their implementation options we will use a simple example based on a newspaper business (Figure 11-6). In this example there are three participants: the newspaper itself, a party acting as a news source, and a customer of the newspaper.

We will examine four use cases (processes) involving these participants:

- The news source delivering a news tip to the newspaper (In-Only)
- The customer subscribing to the newspaper (In-Out)
- The newspaper sending the news electronically to the customer (Out-Only)
- The newspaper sending an offer to the customer that requires a response (Out-In)

Figure 11-6: *Newspaper Example Architecture Pattern*

In-Only Example and Implementation Options

The In-Only example from the newspaper is the news source sending a news tip to the newspaper (Figure 11-7). Here the news source invokes a `receiveTip()` operation provided by the newspaper's service interface.

If you were to implement both the news source and the newspaper as ActiveMatrix components and indicate the news source's reference of the newspaper's service, the result would be a design similar to that shown in Figure 11-8.

For this design you have four transportation options in ActiveMatrix:

- SOAP over HTTP
- SOAP over JMS

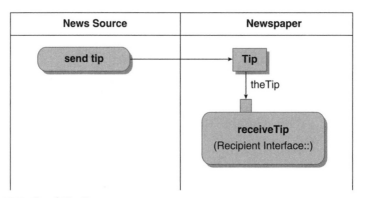

Figure 11-7: *Send Tip Process*

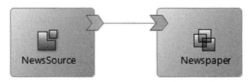

Figure 11-8: *ActiveMatrix Design for Send Tip Process*

- SOAP over ActiveMatrix Virtualization
- XML over JMS

The first of these options uses HTTP as a transport. The implication is that both parties need to be active simultaneously in order for an interaction to occur. The SOAP over JMS and XML over JMS options, because they use a JMS server as a communications intermediary, make it possible for the news source to send the tip when the newspaper is not actively receiving communications. The JMS server will forward the message when the newspaper becomes active.

Despite the fact that ActiveMatrix Virtualization also uses JMS as its underlying communications mechanism, it will not be able to forward a message if the newspaper is not active at the time it is sent. For an explanation, see the "ActiveMatrix Virtualization Transport Limitations" sidebar.

There are five implementation types that would be appropriate for the News Source: TIBCO ActiveMatrix BusinessWorks, Java, C++, Spring, and WebApp. There are four that would be appropriate for the Newspaper: BusinessWorks, Java, C++, and Spring. Note that WebApp would not be appropriate since its input is just the raw HTTP protocol.

ActiveMatrix Virtualization Transport Limitations

When the ActiveMatrix Virtualization transport is used, ActiveMatrix determines the routing between the service consumer and service provider. If the two parties are on different nodes (or if directed by policy), this communication will occur via the JMS server being automatically administered by ActiveMatrix.

When both parties are active, the communications will occur as expected. However, when one or both parties are stopped or undeployed, or the node is stopped, the JMS destination being used for communications between them will be destroyed and any pending messages will be lost.

In-Out Example and Implementation Options

There are two variations on the In-Out pattern: synchronous and asynchronous. In the synchronous pattern, the service consumer (the Subscriber in the example) waits for the response from the service provider (the Newspaper). In the asynchronous variation, the service consumer does not have to wait for the response. Since there are significant differences between these variations in both behavior and implementation options, they will be discussed separately.

Synchronous Variation

The subscribe In-Out process, implemented as a synchronous interaction, is shown in Figure 11-9. The subscriber is invoking the `subscribe()` operation on the newspaper, sending a `SubscribeRequest` and expecting a `SubscribeResponse` in return. In the synchronous variation, the subscriber is actively waiting for the response.

If both subscriber and newspaper were to be implemented as ActiveMatrix components, the result would be a design similar to Figure 11-10.

For this design you have four transportation options in ActiveMatrix:

- SOAP over HTTP
- SOAP over JMS
- SOAP over ActiveMatrix Virtualization
- XML over JMS

For this synchronous variation, the assumption is that both parties are active for the duration of the exchange. The loss of communications or

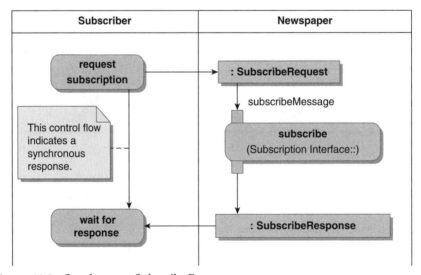

Figure 11-9: *Synchronous Subscribe Process*

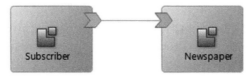

Figure 11-10: *ActiveMatrix Design for Subscribe Process*

the restart of either party may cause exceptions, and both parties should be designed to handle these exceptions gracefully.

There are five implementation types that would be appropriate for the subscriber: BusinessWorks, Java, C++, Spring, and WebApp. There are four that would be appropriate for the Newspaper: BusinessWorks, Java, C++, and Spring. Note that WebApp would not be appropriate since its input is just the raw HTTP protocol.

Asynchronous Variations

There are actually two asynchronous variations for a request-reply exchange. One is the checkpoint pattern shown in Figure 11-11. In this pattern the requestor does not necessarily wait for the reply, but generally must take steps to ensure that, when the reply arrives, it is in a position to handle it. This generally means creating a *checkpoint*, a

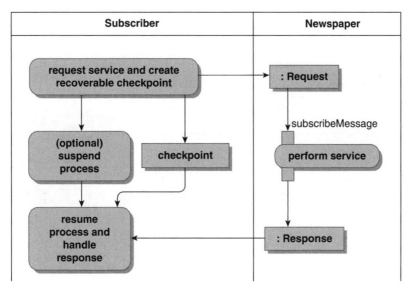

Figure 11-11: *Checkpoint Asynchronous In-Out Pattern*

recoverable snapshot of the requestor's state. In addition, the requestor (in this case the Subscriber) must be implemented in such a way that, should the requestor be halted for any reason, it is resurrected from the checkpoint and is ready to receive the response. Optionally, the process may be suspended to free up resources while waiting for the response.

The checkpoint asynchronous In-Out pattern is typically used when the performance of the requested service is expected to take significant time (minutes or longer). The idea is that, because of the long wait, there is a reasonable possibility that the requestor may be interrupted and you do not want the interruption to adversely impact the execution of the business process. Note, however, that this pattern ties up some resources for each outstanding request.

The other major variation is the third-party asynchronous In-Out pattern shown in Figure 11-12. Here the response is handled by a third party, either a different thread in the requesting process or a completely independent application. In this case there is usually a need for some additional communications between the party sending the request and the party receiving the response.

This additional communication conveys the context information required to handle the response. The content of this context varies from solution to solution, but typically includes information such as:

- Notification that there is an outstanding request. This information (in conjunction with a response-time SLA) enables the response handler to determine when responses are missing or overdue.

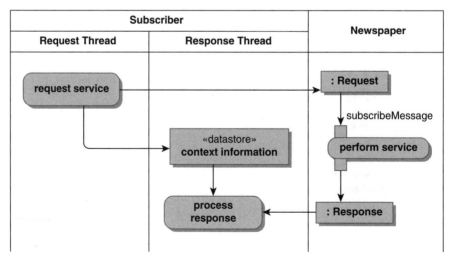

Figure 11-12: *Third-Party Asynchronous In-Out Pattern*

- An identifier for the request that will be returned as part of the response. This allows the response handler to correlate a particular request-response pair.
- Information about the nature of the request needed to properly handle the response. This can be the information itself or a reference to a location (database, file, etc.) in which this information can be found.

The communication of the context information is a design task that should not be overlooked when selecting this pattern. It always requires design and implementation work.

At present the only transport in ActiveMatrix that can support these asynchronous interaction patterns is XML over JMS. When using this transport, the JMSCorrelationID should be used in the request to uniquely identify the request. The value for this field is provided by the requestor and should be returned in the JMSCorrelationID field of the response. Also required is the JMSReplyTo field in the request. Its value should indicate the JMS destination to which the response should be sent.

There are four implementation types that would be appropriate for the subscriber: BusinessWorks, Java, C++, and Spring. The Business Works implementation type is particularly well suited to implementing the request side (e.g., the subscriber) of the checkpoint asynchronous In-Out pattern, as all the mechanisms required for checkpointing and recovery are provided as part of the product. There are four that would be appropriate for the Newspaper: BusinessWorks, Java, C++, and Spring. Note that WebApp would not be appropriate for either role since its input is just the raw HTTP protocol.

Out-Only Example and Implementation Options

The process for delivering the newspaper is shown in Figure 11-13. This Out-Only interaction is inherently asynchronous—the Subscriber is not actively waiting for the paper to be delivered.

The only ActiveMatrix transport that can support this pattern today is XML over JMS.

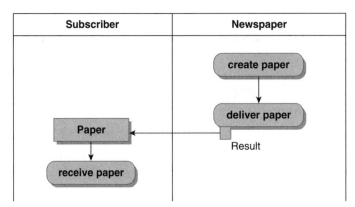

Figure 11-13: *Deliver Paper Process*

The Out-Only pattern is, unfortunately, not well represented in the current version of the SCA notation.[1] The closest you can come in the present notation is the design shown in Figure 11-14. There are two problems with this representation. One is that the diagram implies that it is the subscriber providing the service and the newspaper referencing the service, when in reality the opposite is true. The other is that, for most publications, it is unlikely that the wiring between the Out-Only service provider and service consumer would be done at design time. In other words, it is unlikely that you would ever show both the service provider and service consumer in the same SCA composite. Instead, this wiring would be done either at deployment time or at run time.

What you would create in ActiveMatrix today (until such time as the SCA Event Processing Specification is completed) is a composite containing just the service provider (Figure 11-15). Note that the

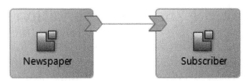

Figure 11-14: *Inappropriate Attempt to Represent Out-Only Pattern in Present SCA Notation*

---

1. The SCA Event Processing Specification is presently under development (see www.osoa.org).

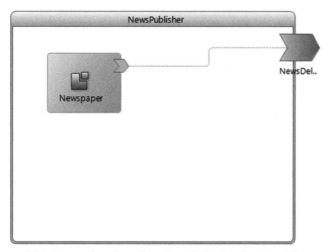

Figure 11-15: *SCA Approximation of an Out-Only Service Provider*

composite shows a reference to the service; the reason is that when you generate implementations, references generate outbound calls, which is consistent with the design intent. This structure (the component referencing the service) can be incorporated into any composite wishing to send Out-Only notifications.

Similarly, you would create the service consumer as a composite with a promoted service (Figure 11-16). From an implementation perspective, this is appropriate since, when you generate the implementation, the generated structure will be appropriate for an inbound call. This structure (the service and its association with a component) can be incorporated into any composite that wishes to receive Out-Only notifications from a service provider.

There is a bit of hidden JMS administrative configuration required to connect the two parties in this pattern. The JMS destination must be created (or the JMS server must be configured to auto-create destinations), and both parties must be configured to use the same destination. This is generally straightforward when the configuration is done at deployment time, but dynamic connection at runtime will require extra design work. For example, if you wanted to have a subscriber dynamically create the subscription, the `subscribe()` operation would have to return the JMS destination and the subscriber would have to have code to alter its configuration to receive messages from this destination.

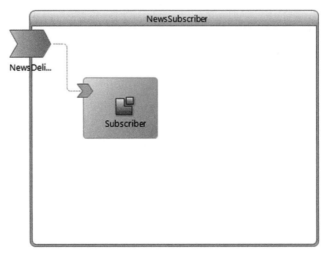

Figure 11-16: *SCA Approximation of an Out-Only Service Consumer*

There are five implementation types that would be appropriate for the newspaper: BusinessWorks, Java, C++, Spring, and WebApp. There are four that would be appropriate for the subscriber: BusinessWorks, Java, C++, and Spring. Note that WebApp would not be appropriate for the subscriber since its input is just the raw HTTP protocol.

Out-In Example and Implementation Options

The process of the newspaper making an offer to a subscriber and then handling the response is shown in Figure 11-17. The interactions here are, by definition, asynchronous: Neither party is actively waiting for an input. Furthermore, the service provider (the newspaper) will likely have separate threads (or applications) for sending the offers and processing the responses. Consequently, there will likely be a need to communicate context information between these two threads as was discussed in the earlier asynchronous In-Out example.

As with the Out-Only pattern, the only suitable protocol and transport combination available in ActiveMatrix is XML over JMS. The SCA design would be similar to that discussed in the Out-Only example, and the JMSCorrelationID and JMSReplyTo properties would have to be used as described in the Asynchronous In-Out example.

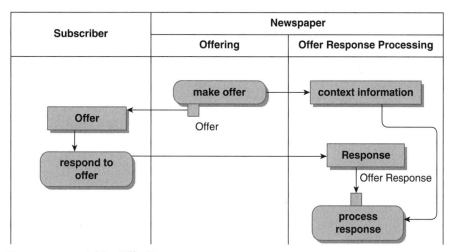

Figure 11-17: *Make Offer Process*

There are five implementation types that would be appropriate for the newspaper: BusinessWorks, Java, C++, and Spring. There are four that would be appropriate for the subscriber: BusinessWorks, Java, C++, and Spring. Note that WebApp would not be appropriate for either role since its input is just the raw HTTP protocol.

Summary

There are four basic message exchange patterns between two parties: In-Only, In-Out, Out-Only, and Out-In. The In-Only pattern and the synchronous variation of the In-Out pattern have many protocol and transport options in ActiveMatrix, including SOAP over HTTP, JMS, and ActiveMatrix Virtualization as well as XML over JMS. The BusinessWorks, Java, C++, Spring, and WebApp implementation types are all suitable for the service-consumer side of these interactions, while the BusinessWorks, Java, C++, and Spring implementation types are appropriate for the service-provider side.

The asynchronous variation of the In-Out pattern and the Out-Only and Out-In patterns all involve asynchronous interactions. At present, the only suitable protocol and transport combination in ActiveMatrix for asynchronous interactions is XML over JMS. For the asynchronous In-Out and Out-In, the JMSCorrelationID and JMSReplyTo properties should be used to correlate the request and reply messages and indicate the JMS destination to which the replies should be sent. For these patterns, the BusinessWorks, Java, C++, and Spring implementation types are all suitable for both parties.

Chapter 12

Event-Driven Interaction Patterns

In the previous chapters we examined four different ways in which two parties might interact, but without asking why they were interacting. For the In-Out and Out-In patterns, the reason is obvious (Figure 12-1a): One party is sending a request to the other and expecting a response. For the In-Only and Out-Only interactions, however, there are two possibilities. The first is that one party is sending a request to the other (Figure 12-1b). The second is that one party is simply sending a notification of some kind to the other (Figure 12-1c).

This seemingly innocuous difference between a request and a notification is, in fact, quite important: It reflects an entirely different style of interaction. Requests are always directed to an identified party and direct that party to take some specific action. Notifications, on the other hand, are simply announcements—and are not necessarily directed at any particular party. In fact, the notification may go to multiple parties (Figure 12-2). It is up to the party receiving the announcement to decide what, if anything, needs to be done.

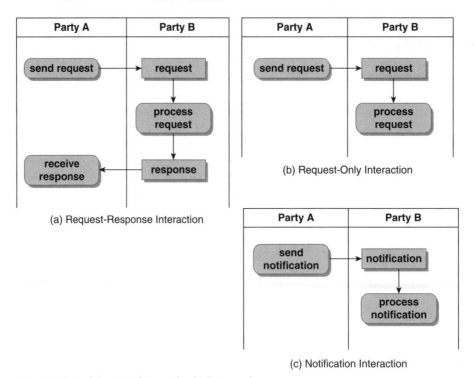

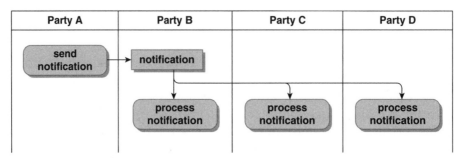

(a) Request-Response Interaction

(b) Request-Only Interaction

(c) Notification Interaction

Figure 12-1: *Message Semantics in Interactions*

Figure 12-2: *Notifications Delivered to Multiple Parties*

The Pub-Sub Architecture Pattern

The idea that a communication—a message—might not be directed to any party gives rise to the notion of an *event-driven interaction*. The *publication* of the message constitutes the announcement of an event, and

Figure 12-3: *Pub-Sub Architecture Pattern*

parties wishing to receive the event obtain a *subscription* for that type of message. The result is the publication-subscription paradigm, often abbreviated as *pub-sub*.

The pub-sub paradigm requires an intermediate communications channel as shown in Figure 12-3. This channel serves several purposes:

- It provides facilities for parties to publish messages.
- It provides facilities for parties to subscribe to messages.
- It directs individual messages to the parties that have subscribed to those messages.
- It acts as a buffer between the publishers and subscribers.

Although file systems and databases can be used as pub-sub communications channels, the most common type of channel is a messaging system. The TIBCO Enterprise Message Service (EMS) is an example of a messaging system designed expressly for this purpose. At its core, it provides the standardized facilities of a Java Messaging Service (JMS).

In JMS, individual channels are referred to as destinations. Publishers send messages to destinations, and a message sent to a destination constitutes an event. Subscribers connect to the EMS server and indicate the destinations to which they would like to subscribe. When a message is published, it is delivered to the appropriate subscriber(s).

Queue Semantics

JMS offers two types of destinations, each with a distinctly different message delivery paradigm: queues and topics. A message sent to a queue is delivered to a single subscriber, regardless of how many subscribers there are for the queue (Figure 12-4).

A queue is generally used to deliver requests as opposed to announcements. In this case, the publisher is the service consumer and the subscriber is the service provider. A channel used in this manner is an example of an In-Only interaction.

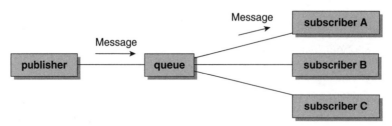

Figure 12-4: *Queue Delivery Semantics*

The reason for having more than one subscriber would be to distribute the load for handling the messages. This means that each of the subscribers does exactly the same thing with the messages. The semantics governing which of the subscribers receives each message depends upon the implementation of the queue. The default EMS semantics is that messages are distributed in a round-robin manner among active subscribers.

Note that distributing load in this manner does not guarantee that messages will be processed in the order in which they were published and delivered. One subscriber may receive a message but not finish processing it before another subscriber finishes processing a subsequent message. There are a number of design patterns that can be used to handle such situations, but a discussion of these patterns is beyond the scope of this book and is addressed in *Architecting Composite Applications and Services with TIBCO*[1].

When a queue is used to deliver requests, replies may be required. To facilitate this, EMS provides several options for returning reply messages to the publisher. These configuration options are described in the product manual. A channel used in this manner is an example of an In-Out interaction.

Queues generally retain messages until they have been delivered. EMS provides several options for persisting messages so that they are not lost in the event of a server restart. Again, these are described in the product manual.

---

1. Paul C. Brown, *Architecting Composite Applications and Services with TIBCO®*, coming soon from Addison-Wesley.

Topic Semantics

When a message is published to a topic, in contrast to a queue, it is delivered to all subscribers (Figure 12-5). Topics are typically used to deliver notifications (announcements) rather than requests. A channel used in this manner is an example of the Out-Only pattern.

Sometimes notifications require responses, as in the previous chapter's example of a newspaper extending an offer to a subscriber that requires a response. To support this, EMS provides facilities to route replies back to the publisher if required. A channel used in this manner is an example of the Out-In pattern in which a single output message constitutes a blanket request to all subscribers.

By default, messages are delivered only to those subscribers that happen to be connected at the time the message is published and then the message is discarded. By exception, subscribers can declare their subscriptions to be *durable*. When there are durable subscribers, EMS will retain messages until those subscribers come back online and have received their messages.

Bridge Semantics

If you examine the design intent of individual messages, some messages are explicit announcements of business events, while others serve as requests or replies. However, broadly speaking, the sending of any message is, in itself, an event. For example, sending a request from one system to another and sending the reply by the second system are two events that occur in the interaction between those two systems.

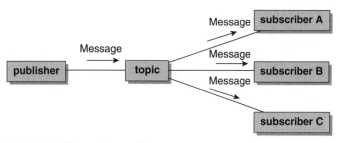

Figure 12-5: *Topic Delivery Semantics*

When you are monitoring a system to see whether it is behaving properly (or for other purposes), these events are the pieces of raw data that serve as the basis for the monitoring. Since individual raw events observed at this level may or may not have business significance, they are often referred to as technical events. Understanding the business meaning of such events is the world of complex event processing.

Complex event processing begins with the capture of technical events. Some of these technical events are the sending of messages, while others may be changes to database records or changes to files. Recognizing and capturing these events is an essential element of complex event processing. Mechanisms for recognizing changes in files and databases are discussed in Chapter 15. For now we will focus our attention on recognizing and capturing messages.

If a message is being published to a topic, capturing the message is as simple as adding a subscriber to the topic. However, if the message is being published to a queue, you can't just add another subscriber because you will disrupt the normal delivery of the message.

EMS provides a facility that can be used to capture copies of messages being published to queues (and topics, for that matter): the *bridge* (Figure 12-6). EMS allows you to create a one-way bridge between any pair of topics and queues. When a message is published to the source destination of the bridge (the queue in the figure), EMS makes a copy of the message and places it in the target destination of the bridge (the topic in the figure).

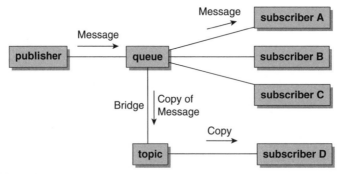

Figure 12-6: *Bridge Message Delivery Semantics*

Other Sources of Events

Most of the discussion in this chapter has focused on messages, since they are the most common mechanism for distributing information about events. However, in many cases the actual event you are looking for may not be a message at all. In these cases, you will most likely need to select a mechanism for recognizing the event and generating a message that can be used to communicate information about the event. Two of the most common examples are database and file changes, both of which are discussed in Chapter 15.

Summary

When two components interact, each interaction represents one of three things: a request for something to be done, a reply to such a request, or an announcement that some business event has occurred.

In contrast to requests and replies, announcements are not necessarily being delivered to a single recipient: It is reasonable to want an announcement to be sent to multiple parties. This sending of a single message to multiple parties gives rise to the pub-sub architecture pattern.

The pub-sub pattern involves a third party providing a communications channel between the publishers and subscribers. The TIBCO Enterprise Message Service (EMS) provides JMS communications capabilities that are well-suited to this channel role.

Messages in JMS are published to destinations, and subscribers receive messages from those destinations. JMS provides two different types of destinations, queues and topics, each with different message delivery semantics. A queue will deliver a message to exactly one subscriber and will retain the message until it has been delivered. Queues are well-suited to request and request-reply interactions. A topic will deliver a message to all subscribers who are connected at the time the message is published. Topics are well-suited to pub-sub (broadcast) interactions.

There are times when it is desirable to treat a queue-based request (or reply) as an event (announcement) in its own right. The EMS bridge provides the means for automatically making a copy of a message when it is delivered and placing the copy in a target topic or queue. This lets you make a copy of the request (or reply) and deliver it to another destination without disrupting the original interaction.

Chapter 13

ActiveMatrix Policy Framework

Aspect-Oriented Design

Sometimes you need to introduce functionality into a process, but that functionality is not a fundamental part of the mainstream process. As an example, consider the Account Management Service from our earlier discussion of the ATM System architecture (Figure 13-1). To avoid unauthorized access to the service operations, you want to add some control over who is able to call them. In other words, you want to introduce a policy that governs access to the service. However, you'd like to accomplish this without modifying the basic design. Furthermore, you want to keep the concerns associated with access control separate from those of the core business processes. This is the idea behind aspect-oriented design.

Aspect-Oriented Design[1] is an emerging architectural philosophy that seeks to achieve this separation of concerns. Central to the discussion is the idea of a crosscutting concern. A concern is a matter of

---

1. Siobhán Clarke and Elisa Baniassad, *Aspect-Oriented Analysis and Design: The Theme Approach*, Boston: Addison-Wesley (2005).

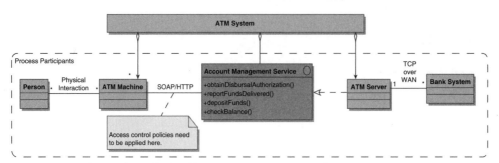

Figure 13-1: *Aspect from the Architecture Pattern Perspective*

interest that applies in multiple situations in the core of the solution.[2] The concern in this example is security, and the core is the architecture pattern.

The idea of *crosscutting* is that the concern needs to be addressed at multiple places in the architecture. In the example, access to each of the service operations needs to be governed. More broadly, access to other components (such as the Bank System) may need to be governed as well. Aspect-oriented design is applicable when there are crosscutting concerns.

Concerns are addressed by adding some behavior that addresses the concern to the design. This behavior, in aspect-oriented terminology, is referred to as *advice*. In the example, the advice is the access control policy that decides whether or not access should be granted. The encapsulation of the advice (added behavior) along with the specification of where it is to be triggered is referred to as an *aspect*. In the example, the indication that the access control policy needs to be applied to the interactions between the ATM Machine and the Account Management service defines the aspect.

If you examine the mapping of the withdraw cash process onto the architecture pattern shown in Figure 13-2, you can see that there are two aspects in this business process—two places at which access control policies need to be applied.

---

2. To be clear here, we are using the terminology of the asymmetric separation paradigm of aspect-oriented design.

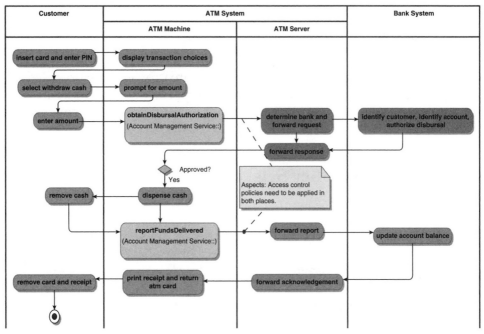

Figure 13-2: *Aspects from the Mapping Perspective*

The ActiveMatrix Policy Approach

The TIBCO ActiveMatrix® Service Bus provides a policy framework that marries the abstractions of aspect-oriented design with the implementation approach of the Service-Component Architecture (SCA) specification. In this framework, advice (added behavior) is specified in the form of policies. The aspect (specification of where the policy is to be applied) is accomplished by associating the policies with specific elements of the SCA design.

The policies and policy templates provided with ActiveMatrix Service Bus address a number of commonly encountered concerns, including:

- Security
- Transactional integrity
- Reliability
- Startup/shutdown sequencing

- Performance tuning
- Location independence

The remainder of this chapter provides an overview of this policy framework and the types of policies that are provided. Be prepared for getting into some details! Understanding how the policies tie in with the core application functionality requires getting under the covers a bit.

Policies and Policy Sets

Policy

The term *policy*, as used in the context of ActiveMatrix Service Bus, refers to a rule governing some aspect of application execution. One generally familiar usage of policies is to govern access to services by authenticating users and authorizing their use of the service. Less familiar might be policies that govern message delivery (at least once delivery, at most once delivery), and the start-up sequencing of components and the services upon which they depend.

Policy Sets

Each policy defines a single rule, but often it is necessary to combine two or more policies to describe the intended behavior. Such groupings are referred to as *policy sets*. A policy set can contain one or more policies. Policy sets are the primary artifacts used to administer policies in ActiveMatrix Service Bus.

Policy sets are defined by XML files. Some policy sets are predefined in ActiveMatrix Service Bus and are referred to as embedded policy sets. You cannot view the XML defining these policy sets. Other policy sets are defined by XML files that you provide. These are referred to as external (i.e., outside the ActiveMatrix Service Bus product) policy sets.

Policy sets can be applied to any SCA element: component, service, reference, or composite. We will see later how policy sets are associated with these elements.

The TIBCO ActiveMatrix Service Bus policy implementation conforms to the SCA Policy Framework V1.00.[3]

---

3. www.osoa.org/display/Main/Service+Component+Architecture+Specifications

Table 13-1 lists the policy sets provided with the ActiveMatrix Service Bus product as of this writing.

Table 13-1: *Policy Sets Provided with TIBCO ActiveMatrix Service Bus*

Policy Set	Description
At Least Once	This policy set ensures that the messaging bus attempts to deliver each message to its destination at least once.
At Most Once	This policy set ensures that the messaging bus attempts to deliver each message to its destination at most once.
Managed Transaction	This policy set starts a managed transaction before running a composite or component, so its operations execute in a transaction environment.
Prepare Before Undeploy	This policy set ensures Administrator does not un-deploy a composite or component until the composite or component explicitly confirms that its preparations are complete.
Secure Virtualization	This policy set ensures that a service receives all messages from the messaging bus using SSL.
Start Service First	This policy set ensures that when a reference is wired to a service, the provider component starts before the referencing component starts.
Threading	This policy set ensures that message sending and dispatch operations use a thread pool.
Transacted One-Way	This policy set ensures delivery of one-way messages by wrapping message operations (send or receive) within transactions.
Virtualize	This policy set ensures that messages travel through the messaging bus, blocking potential optimization, while enabling beneficial side effects of the messaging bus.

Continues

Table 13-1: *Policy Sets Provided with TIBCO ActiveMatrix Service Bus (Continued)*

Policy Set	Description
WS-Addressing for References	This policy set ensures that a reference sends messages with WS-Addressing semantics.
WS-Addressing for Services	This policy set ensures that a service receives messages with WS-Addressing semantics.
WS-Reliable Messaging	This policy set ensures that a service receives messages or a reference sends messages with WS-RM semantics. For details, see the Web Services Reliable Messaging specification.

Policy Set Templates

Many policies employ values that may need to change from application to application. For example, if you want to do role-based authorization, the list of roles authorized to access a particular service interface will vary from service to service.

To facilitate the use of such policies, ActiveMatrix Service Bus provides a number of *policy set templates* (referred to as simply *policy templates* in the product documentation) that contain placeholders for the values. To use these policy set templates, you edit the template XML file and save it. The edited file, with all values supplied, is a complete policy set that can be used as an external policy set. The default location (on Windows) for these templates is:

```
C:\Program Files (x86)\TIBCO\amx-3\amx\3.0\samples\policy\
samples.zip
```

Consider the policy set in Listing 13-1. It contains one policy that defines authorization by role. The policy permits access to all operations when the role matches one of the entries in the role list. The template, as provided, has exactly one role: Manager. To use this template, you would replace Manager with a comma-separated list of the roles you want to allow, save this XML file under a new name, and later apply it in a project (this last part will be described later in this chapter).

Listing 13–1: *Samples\AuthorizationByRole\AllOperationsAllowedForRole.*
policysets

```
<sca:policySet
  name="AuthorizationByRole_AllOperationsAllowedForRole.role"
  provides="scaext:authorization.role"
  appliesTo="webapp:implementation.web | soapbt:binding.soap.service">

  <wsp:Policy template="tpt:AuthorizationByRole"
   xmlns:tpt="http://xsd.tns.tibco.com/governance/policy/template/2009"
   xmlns:xacml="urn:oasis:names:tc:xacml:2.0:policy:schema:os">
   <!-- Authorize all operations for users with specific roles -->
    <wsp:All>
      <wsp:Policy>
        <wsp:All>
          <tpa:Authorization>
            <tpa:ByRole>
              <tpa:Default>
                <xacml:Rule Effect="Permit" RuleId="">
                <xacml:Description>All operations allowed for specific
                  Roles</xacml:Description>
                  <xacml:Condition>
                    <xacml:Apply FunctionId="is-in">
                      <!-- Replace the value "Manager" below with a
                       valid Role list. Role names are comma separated.
                       -->
                      <xacml:AttributeValue DataType="xsd:string">
                        Manager
                      </xacml:AttributeValue>
                    </xacml:Apply>
                  </xacml:Condition>
                </xacml:Rule>
              </tpa:Default>
            </tpa:ByRole>
          </tpa:Authorization>
        </wsp:All>
      </wsp:Policy>
    </wsp:All>
  </wsp:Policy>
</sca:policySet>
```

Some of the categories and templates provided with the Active-
Matrix Service Bus include:

- Authentication: basic LDAP authentication; token-based LDAP
  authentication; SAML authentication (signed and unsigned)

- Authorization by Role:all operations allowed for role; authenticated
  users only; everyone allowed; nobody allowed; specific operation
  allowed for all roles; specific operation allowed for specific role

- Credential Mapping: fixed credential mapping; role-based credential mapping; SAML credential mapping signed; SAML credential mapping unsigned
- WSS Consumer: add username, token, timestamp, sign, and encrypt
- WSS Provider: authenticate username, SAML, token; decrypt

Policy Applicability

If you look over the types of policy sets and think about the different types of elements in an SCA design (components, services, references, and composites), it becomes obvious that certain types of policy sets only apply to certain types of elements. This concept is formalized in the @appliesTo attribute of an SCA policy set in which you can specify the type of element to which the policy set applies.

While you are unlikely to be creating policy sets from scratch (and therefore setting the values of @appliesTo attributes), the concept is still important. It allows you, for example, to associate multiple policy sets with a composite and have those policy sets automatically apply themselves to the appropriate elements within that composite.

Policy Enforcement Points

A policy enforcement point is, as the name implies, the place at which policies are actually enforced. The policy enforcement point in the TIBCO ActiveMatrix Service Bus is the node. Within each node we can be even more specific when it comes to access control policies. Referring back to Figure 9-6, every access to every implementation, binding, and communication resource can be governed by policies. This provides an extremely secure environment for computing and communications.

Associating Policy Sets with Design Elements

As of this writing, policy sets can only be associated with design elements at design time. In a future release, it is planned that policy sets may be associated at deployment time as well.

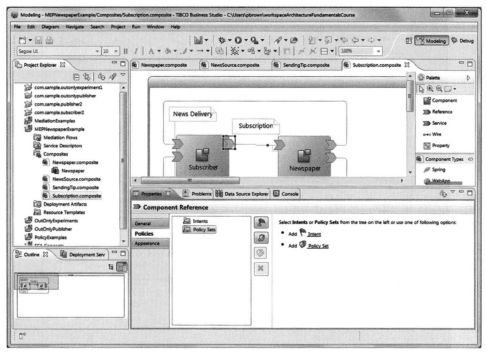

Figure 13-3: *Associating Policy Sets with a Reference at Design Time*

The mechanics of associating a policy set with a reference are illustrated in Figure 13-3. You select the reference, and in the Properties tab below select the Policies sub-tab. You select the Policy Sets icon, which becomes highlighted. At this point you can select Add a Policy Set.

Once you click on the Policy Set icon, the dialog shown in Figure 13-4 will appear. From this dialog you can either select an embedded policy set or reference an external policy set. You should consult the product manual for further information.

Worth mentioning here is the fact that the external policy set you reference does not have to be in the project in which the composite is being defined: It can be in another project. This creates the opportunity to place policy sets in a project that is subsequently used (referenced) by a number of other projects. This can greatly simplify the creation and management of policies.

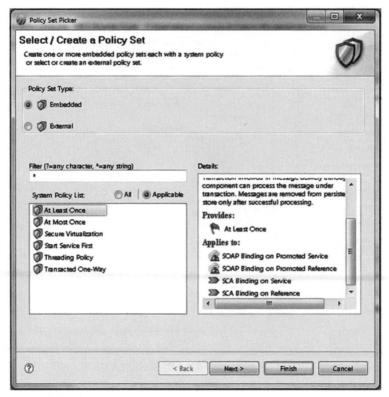

Figure 13-4: *Selecting or Creating a Policy Set*

Policies That Access External Systems

Many policies require access to external systems such as LDAP. When this happens, the architecture pattern of Figure 13-5 must be employed. The actual access to the external system is managed by a special type of component known as a governance agent. When you create the governance agent (which will be described in a moment) you will give it a name, and it is this name that will appear in the policy set.

The governance agent, in turn, will require an ActiveMatrix Service Bus shared resource. This resource defines the configuration of the communications channel that will be used to communicate with the external system. When you configure the governance agent, you will have to provide the name of the shared resource that defines the communications channel.

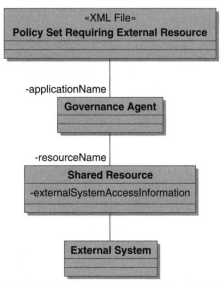

Figure 13-5: *Architecture Pattern for Accessing External Systems*

Figure 13-6 shows the general procedure for accessing an external system from a policy set. At the time you are designing the solution requiring the policy set, you need to copy the template policy set into a project (remember, it doesn't have to be the project containing the design) and edit the governance agent name that appears in the policy set. You'll have to remember this name because you'll need it later. Then you can reference the policy set from the design element to which it applies and generate the distributed application archive (DAA).

In the administrator you need to create the shared resource template that defines the connection to the external system. The Active-Matrix Administrator provides dialogs for creating resource templates for all types of external systems referenced in the supplied policy sets. You create the shared resource template by selecting the template type and giving it a name.

Then you create the governance application from the template supplied by ActiveMatrix Service Bus. You name the governance application, taking care to use the same name that you put into the policy set. Next, configure the governance application to reference the shared resource you just created that defines the connection. Finally, you deploy the solution. You create an instance of the shared resource on

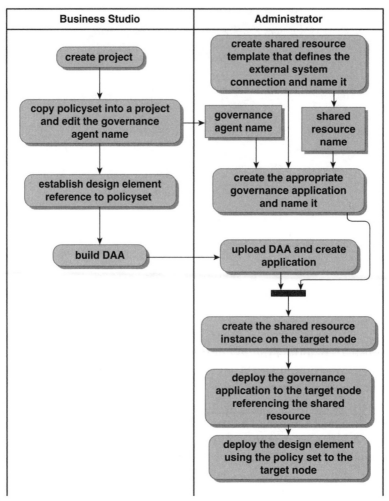

Figure 13-6: *Procedure for Accessing External Systems in a Policy Set*

the target node to which you will deploy the design element using the policy set. You deploy the governance application to the target node, configuring it to use the shared resource instance you just created. Finally, you deploy the design element using the policy set to the target node.

Table 13-2 lists the types of policies provided with ActiveMatrix Service Bus that require access to external systems and the corresponding shared resource templates that must be used.

Table 13-2: *Policy Types Requiring Access to External Systems*

Policies Involving These Features	*Require These Resource Templates*
Signing or Decryption	Identity Provider Keystore Provider
Signature Verification or Encryption	Trust Provider Keystore Provider
Both of the above	Mutual Identity Provider Keystore Provider
WssProvider or WssConsumer	WSS Authentication Provider
LDAP for authentication	LDAP Authentication Provider

An Example: Implementing a Policy Accessing LDAP

Let's take a look at a concrete example in which you want to apply the `BasicAuthenticationWithWebAppUsingLDAP.policysets`.

The first thing to do is to make a copy of the policy set (which is really a template) and edit the governance application name (Listing 13-2). The listing shows this policy set highlighting the governance application name that is to be replaced. For our example, let's call this the `LDAP_Access_Application`. Remember the name—you will need it later!

Listing 13–2: *BasicAuthenticationWithWebAppUsingLDAP.policysets*

```
<?xml version="1.0" encoding="UTF-8"?>
<ep:policySetContainer
  xmlns:ep="http://xsd.tns.tibco.com/amf/models/externalpolicy"
  xmlns:sca="http://www.osoa.org/xmlns/sca/1.0"
  xmlns:scaext="http://xsd.tns.tibco.com/amf/models/sca/extensions"
  xmlns:wsp="http://schemas.xmlsoap.org/ws/2004/09/policy"
  xmlns:tpa="http://xsd.tns.tibco.com/governance/policy/action/2009"
  xmlns:tpc="http://xsd.tns.tibco.com/governance/policy/common/2009"
  xmlns:jmsbt="http://xsd.tns.tibco.com/amf/models/sca/bindingtype/jms"
  xmlns:soapbt="http://xsd.tns.tibco.com/amf/models/sca/binding/soap"
  xmlns:webapp="http://xsd.tns.tibco.com/amf/models/sca/implementation
type/webapp"
  xmlns:wssp="http://docs.oasis-open.org/ws-sx/ws-securitypolicy/200702
    targetNamespace="http://www.example.com/policySets">
"
```

```
<sca:policySet name="BasicAuthenticationPolicySet"
  appliesTo="soapbt:binding.soap.service.http|webapp:implementation.
web"
  provides="scaext:clientAuthentication.basic">
  <wsp:Policy template="tpt:BasicAuthentication"
    xmlns:tpt="http://xsd.tns.tibco.com/governance/policy/template/
2009">
    <wsp:All>
      <wsp:Policy>
        <wsp:All>
          <tpa:AuthenticationByJaas>
            <tpa:SecurityToken>
              <tpa:ExactlyOne>
                <!-- Enforce HTTP basic authentication -->
                <wssp:HttpBasicAuthentication/>
              </tpa:ExactlyOne>
            </tpa:SecurityToken>
            <!-- Replace the sample ResourceInstance attribute value
              "DefaultLdapAsp" below with the name of a TIBCO
              ActiveMatrix Governance Agent application that
              references an "LDAP Authentication" resource instance.
            -->
            <tpa:SharedResourceLoginModule
              ResourceInstance="DefaultLdapAsp"/>
          </tpa:AuthenticationByJaas>
        </wsp:All>
      </wsp:Policy>
    </wsp:All>
  </wsp:Policy>
</sca:policySet>
</ep:policySetContainer>
```

There is an unfortunate terminology conflict in this file that may lead to confusion. The name of the element being edited is SharedResourceLoginModule, and the name of the attribute being edited is ResourceInstance. Despite these names, the value you are editing refers to the governance application, not the shared resource template that defines the connection to the external system.

After the policy set has been created, you can associate it with the service or composite you want it to govern. Note that if you associate the policy set with a composite, it will apply to all SOAP bindings and WebApp HTTP interfaces in that composite.

Over in the administrator you need to create the shared resource template that defines the connection to the LDAP server. The starting point for this is the Shared Objects menu on the administrator (Figure 13-7).

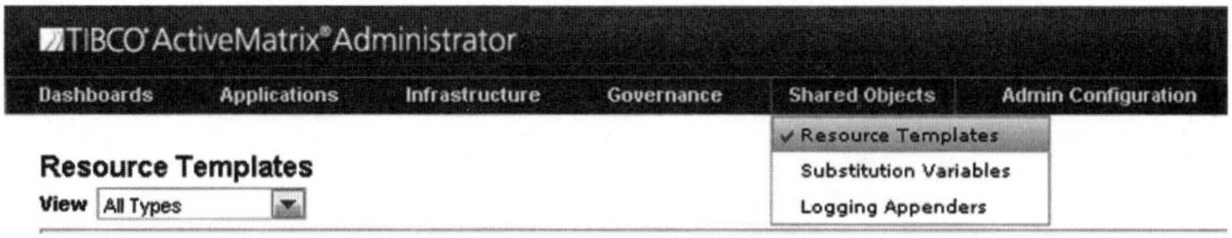

Figure 13-7: *Starting Point for Defining the LDAP Shared Resource*

This will bring up the Resource Templates dialog (Figure 13-8). If the resource template you are looking for (in this case the LDAP Connection) is not in the list, click on the +New icon.

This will bring up the Add Resource Template dialog (Figure 13-9). Select the `LDAP Connection` in the Type pull-down and enter a name for the resource template. Here we have given it the name `LDAP_Connection_A`. Set the parameters appropriately and click Save.

Next, you need to create the governance application that will manage the interactions with the LDAP server. In the administrator, click on Applications on the menu bar and then +New. This will bring up the dialog of Figure 13-10. Enter `LDAP_Access_Application`, the application name that you put in the policy set earlier. Make sure the An existing application template button is selected and click Next.

This will bring up the dialog in Figure 13-11. Scroll down and select the LDAP authentication governance agent and select Next.

On the following dialog, select Done with Application Setup. From this point on, the remainder of the procedure is the same as for any other application being deployed: Create the needed shared resource

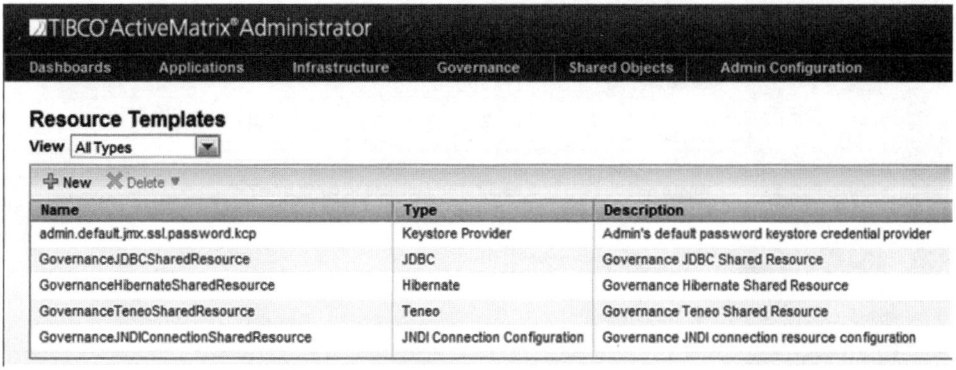

Figure 13-8: *Resource Templates Dialog*

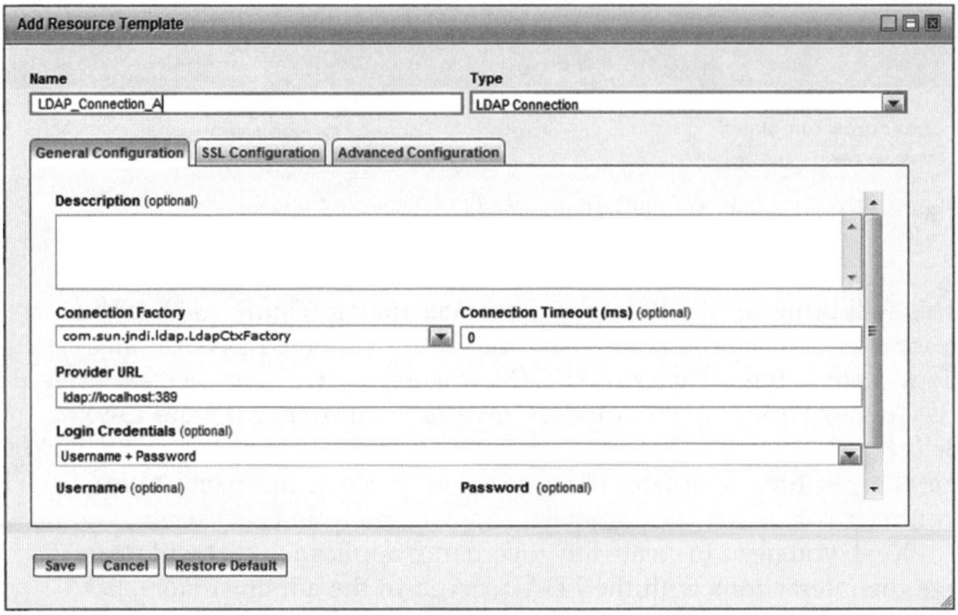

Figure 13-9: *Add Resource Template Dialog*

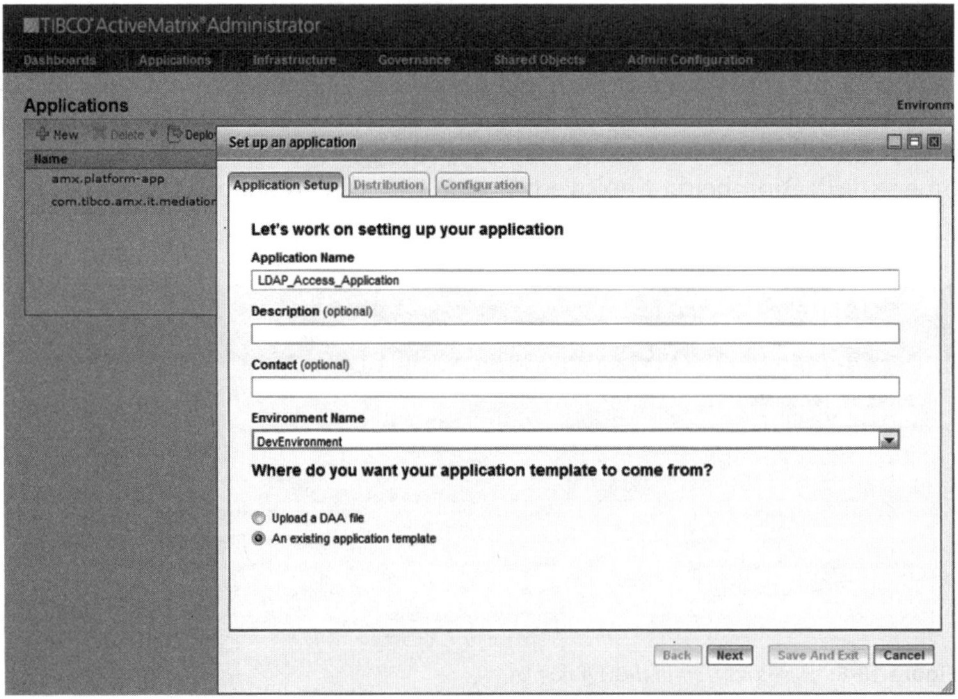

Figure 13-10: *Creating the LDAP_Access_Application*

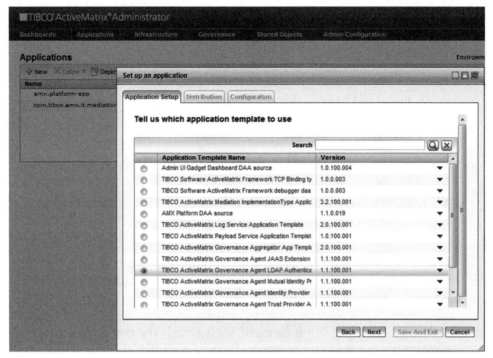

Figure 13-11: *Selecting the LDAP Governance Application Template*

on the target node; deploy the governance agent to the node, configuring it to use the shared resource; and deploy the solution elements requiring the governance agent.

Policy Intents

Policy intents are used to describe the abstract policy requirements of a component or the requirements of interactions among components represented by services and references.[4] An intent expresses a need that eventually must be satisfied by a policy set.

ActiveMatrix Service Bus defines policy intents in a number of categories, including:

---

4. SCA Policy Framework section 1.2.2, www.osoa.org/display/Main/Service+Comp onent+Architecture+Specifications

- Security: client and server authentication; authorization; credential mapping; provider and consumer confidentiality (encryption); provider and consumer integrity (signing)
- Transactions: managed transactions (requires an open transaction); transacted one-way (messages are sent within a transaction and delivered only after the transaction commits)
- Virtualization: secure virtualization (references and services use SSL for communications)
- Reliability: at least once message delivery; at most once message delivery
- LifeCycle: start services first (referenced services must start before the referencing component starts); prepare before un-deploy (component confirms readiness to un-deploy to administrator)

Policy intents are associated with SCA elements at design time (Figure 13-3). Each policy intent has a unique identifier, such as `scaext:clientAuthentication.basic`.

A policy intent is satisfied by associating a policy set that satisfies the intent with the same element with which the intent is associated. Each policy set has a `provides` attribute that lists the intents satisfied by the policy set. For example, if you look at Listing 13-2 you will see the `provides` attribute has the value `scaext:clientAuthentication.basic`.

A policy intent must be satisfied before deployment can complete. As of this writing, the policies that satisfy the intents must be provided at design time. It is intended that in a later ActiveMatrix release the actual association of the policy sets will be possible at deployment time.

Summary

A policy is a rule that governs some aspect of run-time behavior. Policy sets are groups of policies and are the atomic unit of policy administration. Some policy sets are built into the TIBCO ActiveMatrix Service Bus and are referred to as embedded policy sets. Other policy sets are defined by XML files and are referred to as external policy sets. These external policy sets are resources that can be referenced across ActiveMatrix projects.

A policy set template (or simply policy template) is a policy set that requires editing before it can be applied. These edits typically involve supplying values of various types. The resulting edited policy set can then be used as an external policy set in an ActiveMatrix project.

Different policy sets are appropriate for different kinds of design elements. Each policy set declares the type of design element to which it applies. These declarations enable policy sets to be applied to complex elements such as composites and automatically determine the sub-elements to which they apply.

Policies are enforced in ActiveMatrix nodes. Within each node, each component, service, reference, and communication resource has an associated logical policy enforcement point at which access control and communications policies will be enforced.

Policy sets are associated with design elements: components, services, references, and composites. At present, this association is done at design time. In future releases, it will become possible to associate policy sets at deployment time.

Policies that access external systems such as LDAP require special ActiveMatrix Service Bus components, known as governance applications, to mediate the external system interactions. The connection details are specified in a shared resource template. When the design element associated with the policy is deployed, the governance application and shared resource must also be deployed on the same node.

Policy intents are requirement statements about policies that are needed. Each policy intent has a unique identifier, and each policy set lists the intents that it will satisfy. Policy intents are associated with design elements at design time. At present, the corresponding policy sets must also be provided at design time, but in later releases it will become possible to defer the provisioning of the policy sets until deployment time.

Chapter 14

Mediation Patterns

The next set of design patterns we will consider addresses mediation: the insertion of some simple intervening logic between a service consumer and a service provider. As the name implies, mediation activities modify, but do not fundamentally alter, the interactions between the two primary parties. Typical mediation activities include mapping one interface to another, transforming message content, routing requests, and enhancing message content.

Figure 14-1 shows the basic ActiveMatrix mediation architecture pattern that we will discuss. In this pattern the mediator is an ActiveMatrix composite, and it does not matter whether the service consumer and service provider reside within ActiveMatrix or outside the environment. There are variants of this pattern in which the service consumer and/or service provider are also resident within the composite, but these variants become obvious once the basic pattern is understood.

Figure 14-1: *Mediation Architecture Pattern*

Straight-Wire Mapping

The simplest form of mediation is the straight-wire mapping of a service to a reference (Figure 14-2). There are no activities involved in this mediation, only the connection between the service and the reference. A prerequisite for this type of mediation is that the port types (interfaces) of both the service and reference must be identical.

Given the simplicity of this mapping, it might occur to you to ask why you cannot simply wire the composite's service directly to its reference. The answer is that the SCA Assembly Model does not permit such wiring within a composite. A promoted service can only be wired to a service on a component within the composite. Similarly, a promoted reference can only be wired to a reference on a component within the composite. Thus, a component is required in order to implement this mapping.

Any of the ActiveMatrix implementation types could potentially be used for this purpose, but one in particular is designed for this task: the Mediation implementation type. Mediation is a lightweight (small footprint, low overhead) implementation type that is easily configured to perform the most common mediation activities—including straight-through wiring. Figure 14-3 shows a mediation implementation type playing this role in a composite.

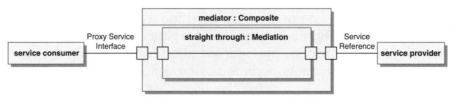

Figure 14-2: *Straight-Wire Architecture Pattern*

Figure 14-3: *Mediation Implementation Type in a Composite*

Mediation Flow Design

Looking into the design of the mediation implementation type (Figure 14-4) you will see that there are different views for the input, output, and fault flows. The input and output flows are exactly what you would expect: straight wires. The mediation input maps directly to the target input and the target output maps directly to the mediation output.

The fault flow, on the other hand, surfaces one of the complexities of mediation: Faults can arise for a number of reasons. The call to the target interface could timeout. The target interface might throw an

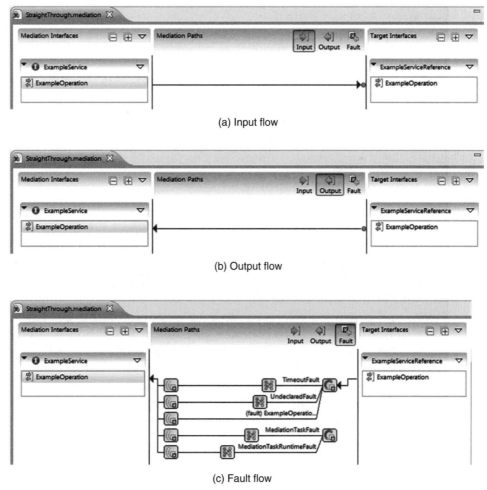

(a) Input flow

(b) Output flow

(c) Fault flow

Figure 14-4: *Mediation Design Interface*

undeclared fault or throw the fault its interface explicitly declares. A task in the mediation flow itself (like one of the mappings in one of the other fault paths!) might throw a fault, or the mediation component as a whole might throw a run-time fault. For now, don't worry about the icons on the paths here; these will be explained in due course.

The mediation implementation type has built-in features for handling all of these variations. If you were to use another implementation type for this or any other mediation purpose you would, at a minimum, have to replicate all of this functionality. This would require considerable design effort. This is the reason for having the mediation implementation type.

Use Case: Access Control

You might be asking yourself why you would ever want to wire a service to a reference in this manner rather than have the service consumer directly access the service provider. The answer is that both the services and references are policy enforcement points. Using this pattern makes it possible to insert access control policies into the dialog between service consumer and service provider. Furthermore, it allows you to hide the actual service provider interface from the service consumer.

Use Case: Transport Mapping

Another situation in which this pattern is useful arises when the service consumer and service provider want to use different transports for the exchange. Both parties use the same SOAP port type (interface) definition, but one may want to use a different transport than the other. Remember that ActiveMatrix provides three SOAP transports: HTTP, JMS, and Virtualization. Using the straight-wire pattern, the promoted service and promoted reference can each be configured to provide a different transport. This is a common situation when in-house service access is being provided via JMS or Virtualization transports but externally exposed services are being provided via HTTP.

A variation on this occurs when you would like to provide the same service via two different transports (Figure 14-5). Here you have two different promoted services, each with a different transport, wired to the same mediation service. The mediation design is exactly the same—only the additional promoted service binding has been added.

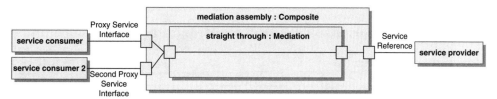

Figure 14-5: *Accessing the Same Service via Two Different Transports*

Content Transformation

The straight-wire pattern required that both parties have identical logical interfaces, but it is to be expected that parties not having identical interfaces will still want to interact. The data transformation architecture pattern (Figure 14-6) provides a solution to this problem. A component within the data transformation composite is providing the data transformation.

Once again, any of the implementation types could be used to implement this component, but it is particularly easy and efficient to use the Mediation implementation type for this purpose. Figure 14-7 shows a mediation flow in which a data transformation activity has been dropped (literally) on the wire between the two service operations. The lower half of the window shows the drag-and-drop configuration of the mapping between the two interfaces. Mappings in the output direction and for faults are configured in a similar manner.

Although the Mediation implementation type is flexible, it is not always suitable for every application. When additional logic is required, such as updates to other systems, the invocation of packaged libraries, or the execution of complex algorithms, other implementation types will likely be more suitable. TIBCO ActiveMatrix Business-Works, for example, provides the design convenience of the Mediation

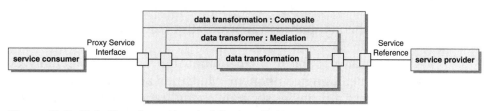

Figure 14-6: *Data Transformation Architecture Pattern*

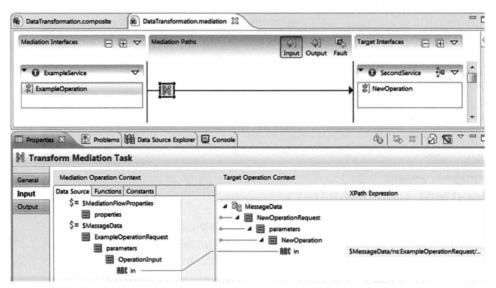

Figure 14-7: *Configuring the Data Transformation in a Mediation Flow*

implementation type coupled with a broad range of communication and functional capabilities. Its power and flexibility warrant first consideration if the requirements exceed the Mediation capabilities.

Data Augmentation

Sometimes you will find that you need information to call the referenced service that is not present in the inbound request. Very often you will need to look up that extra information in an external system and then combine it with the incoming information to create the target service's request. The resulting architecture pattern is shown in Figure 14-8.

For similar reasons, additional work may be required when handling the response and exceptions as well. The full process is shown in Figure 14-9.

Building this composite in ActiveMatrix will yield a design similar to that of Figure 14-10.

Although any of the implementation types could potentially be used for the mediating component, Mediation again simplifies implementation, since it provides separate configurations for the input, output, and exception flows. Figure 14-11 shows an example implementation for the input flow.

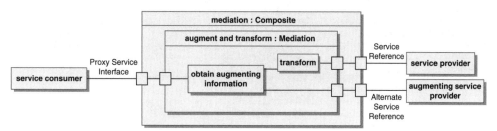

Figure 14-8: *Data Augmentation Architecture Pattern*

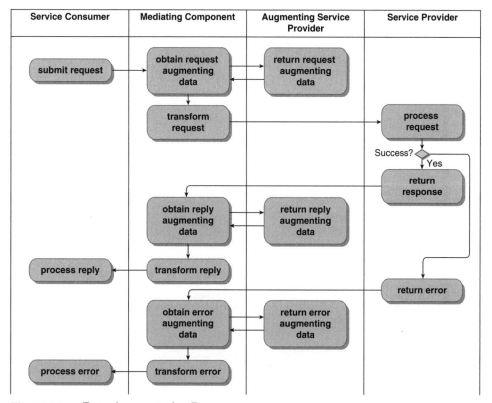

Figure 14-9: *Data Augmentation Process*

The mediation flow design interface provides several activities that can be used to obtain augmenting information. These include:

- A call to a SOAP service operation
- A JDBC query to a database
- A custom Java task

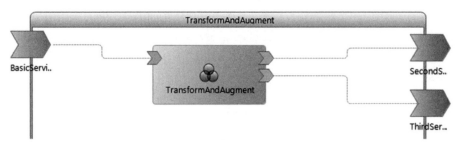

Figure 14-10: *The Data Augmentation Composite*

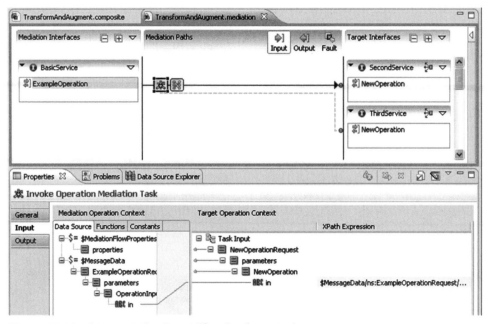

Figure 14-11: *Augmentation Input Flow Implementation*

Routing

In complex environments there may be more than one implementation of a service, or two different services providing essentially the same functionality. In such cases, a request from a service consumer must be routed to the appropriate service provider. The architecture pattern for this is shown in Figure 14-12.

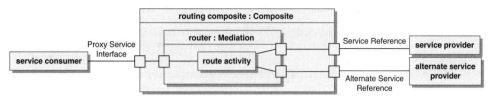

Figure 14-12: *Routing Architecture Pattern*

When you implement this composite in ActiveMatrix the result will be similar to the composite shown in Figure 14-13.

Once again, any of the ActiveMatrix implementation types can be used for the router component, but Mediation is specifically designed for such cases. An example input flow is shown in Figure 14-14. Here, transactions are being routed based on whether they are domestic or foreign. United States transactions are routed to the second service, while all others are routed to the third service. Note that transformations are generally required when routing.

There are three routing options available in the mediation flow. The basic Route activity allows you to define simple conditions on one or more variables. The XPath Route enables you to use XPath expressions and more complex logic to determine the choices.

The third option, dynamic routing, is only available when using the ActiveMatrix Virtualization transport (Figure 14-15). It allows you to compute the name of the service that is going to be invoked. Let's assume that you have a service for each foreign country, with the service named `Transaction.Country`. You also want the ability to dynamically add new countries without having to redesign the mediation flow each time. In this case you would modify the target interface for the "Otherwise" case to be a dynamic service reference. In the "Otherwise" path you would add a Set Dynamic Reference activity to

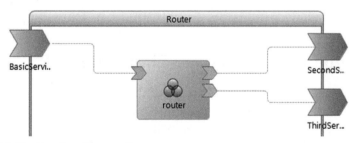

Figure 14-13: *Routing Composite*

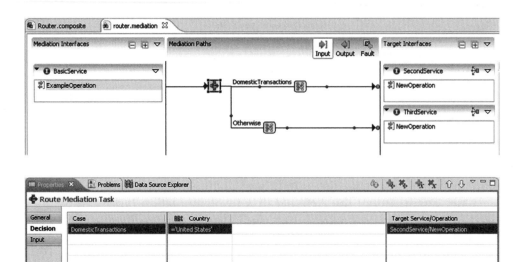

Figure 14-14: *Routing Input Flow Implementation*

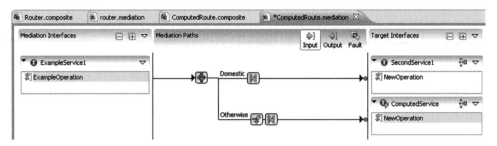

Figure 14-15: *Dynamic Routing*

compute the name of the target service. Of course, you would also want to add an appropriate fault handler for the case in which the target service does not exist.

Mediation Capabilities and Limitations

As this chapter has illustrated, the Mediation implementation type has a broad set of capabilities commonly required when implementing mediation patterns. Its capabilities include:

- Accessing external systems: SOAP operation calls and JDBC database queries
- Making log entries
- Manipulating data: XML parsing, rendering, and validation
- Routing: based on Xpath or other criteria, or dynamically setting reference destinations
- Synthesizing replies
- Managing context between requests and replies
- Throwing faults

The Mediation implementation type does have some limitations. Chief among these is that it can only support the In-Only and In-Out interaction patterns. The use of Out-Only or Out-In patterns thus requires another implementation type to be used.

Summary

Mediation is required when there is logic that must be inserted between a service consumer and a service provider. Mediation logic typically does not produce side-effect changes in other systems as part of the interaction.

The simplest ActiveMatrix mediation pattern is a straight-wire connection between a service consumer and a service provider. This affords the opportunity to change transports and apply access control policies to the interactions. Straight-wire mediation requires that both the consumer and provider have identical logical interfaces. The Mediation implementation type provides the simplest possible implementation of this pattern.

Content transformation is another common mediation requirement. This requirement arises when the interface being used by the service consumer differs from that of the service provider. In such cases both the input and output data structures typically need to be mapped, as well as the exceptions that may be raised. The Mediation data transformation activities provide a simple approach to satisfying such requirements.

Data augmentation is another common requirement. Sometimes data (e.g., an identifier) from the service consumer needs to be cross-referenced to obtain the appropriate data for the service provider. In other cases, additional information needs to be looked up in an external system and added to the service provider input. The Mediation SOAP operation call and JDBC query activities provide convenient means for satisfying these requirements.

Requirements for routing arise when two or more service providers can satisfy a request. In the simplest scenarios, there is information in the input sufficient to determine which service provider should receive the request. In more complex scenarios a lookup in an external system may be necessary to determine the appropriate recipient. The Mediation Route, Xpath Route, and Set Dynamic Reference activities provide flexible mechanisms to implement routing.

The Mediation implementation type provides a broad range of functionality commonly required for mediation. It provides an easy-to-configure interface and efficient execution. However, it can only participate in In-Only and In-Out interaction patterns. Out-Only and Out-In patterns require the use of other implementation types for the mediation role.

Chapter 15

System Access Patterns

It's a pretty sure bet that whatever you implement in TIBCO ActiveMatrix Service Bus is going to have to interact with an external system. This chapter examines the different approaches that can be taken to external system access. It then explores the implementation options for accessing systems, including:

- Direct interaction via an ActiveMatrix-supported protocol (e.g., SOAP service calls)
- Indirect interaction via an ActiveMatrix adapter
- Direct interaction by a component using a non-ActiveMatrix-supported protocol

Approaches to Accessing External Systems

There are four commonly available approaches available for accessing external systems:

- Application Programming Interface (API) interaction
- Database interaction
- File-based interaction
- Protocol-based interaction

Figure 15-1: *External System Interactions*

When considering which approach to employ, you need to consider how the approach works in both the inbound (to the external system) and outbound (from the external system) directions (Figure 15-1). A closely related issue is that of event recognition: recognizing the event that should trigger the interaction. The following sections explore the four interaction options with respect to both the direction of interaction and event recognition.

Application Programming Interface (API) Interaction

An application programming interface (API) is a programming-language interface provided by an application to support interactions with the application. By definition, an API is provided in some pro-gramming languages.

APIs provide a reasonable way to implement interactions in the inbound direction. In the design of your ActiveMatrix component, you (a) recognize that an interaction is required, and (b) call (directly or indirectly) the API provided by the external system.

APIs do not work as well in the outbound direction. Getting an external system to call your code is not straightforward. It typically requires the external system to have a means of registering callbacks, pieces of your code that get called when specific events occur in the external system. Few systems have such a capability.

Database Interaction

Many applications have underlying databases in which they store information. Provided that the schema of the database is understood, it is simple to query the database and extract information. Furthermore, with the addition of a database trigger, you can actually recognize that a change has occurred in the database (i.e., recognize an event) and use the trigger to extract and publish information about the change. Virtually any significant event in the application results in a database change, so this makes it a fairly straightforward process to recognize application events and publish outbound notifications that these events have occurred.

In the inbound direction, however, database interactions have serious limitations. In general, applications have business logic either in the application itself or embedded in stored procedures in the database. It is generally unacceptable to make direct changes to these databases. Thus, database interactions do not provide a good mechanism for inbound communication.

File-Based Interaction

Many older applications (and some newer ones as well) have mechanisms for generating and consuming files. In the inbound direction, applications typically will have a well-defined file format that you can create with an ActiveMatrix component (directly or indirectly). In addition, most have a corresponding command-line interface that you can invoke that will cause the application to consume the file.

In the outbound direction, many applications have the ability to generate files that contain extracts of their information. Many also have a command-line interface that can be invoked to generate this file. Event recognition, however, remains a problem in the outbound direction. Outbound files are typically not generated in response to an event, but rather in response to some external action (e.g., calling the command-line utility) or a scheduled activity. In practice, files are not generated very often and do not serve well as an event-recognition mechanism.

Protocol-Based Interaction

A protocol-based interaction is, logically, the combination of an API with a transport. The SOAP interfaces provided by many modern systems are typical examples.

Protocol-based interactions tend to have the same limitations as API-based interactions: strong in the inbound direction and weak in the outbound direction. Most systems do not have the capability for you to register your protocol-based interface and have it called by the system when a particular event occurs.

The Event Recognition Challenge

Event recognition is a key challenge when interacting with external systems. Business-significant events typically result in changes to these systems, and recognizing these changes is an important means of triggering activity elsewhere when those events occur. In an event-driven enterprise you want to be able to trigger activity upon arrival of a customer, creation of a new account, placement of an order, or change of inventory level. An inability to recognize these events makes it very difficult to trigger work elsewhere.

One historical solution to event recognition has been extract-transform-load (ETL) interactions between systems. Periodically, one system will do a mass extract of information that is subsequently transformed and loaded into a second system. Although some source systems are capable of identifying what has changed since the last extract, others simply extract it all and leave it up to the receiving system to determine what, if anything, has changed.

ETL interactions generally move large amounts of information (particularly when changes are not identified in the source system). Processing large amounts of information is costly, and consequently ETL interactions tend to be performed infrequently. The result can be a delay in event recognition (and action) and data inconsistencies between the systems.

An alternative to ETL interactions is to use database triggers to initiate the information exchange between systems. The database trigger recognizes the change and initiates an outbound communication that can trigger work elsewhere. With this approach only the changes are published, and the published information can be limited to only that which is required elsewhere. The TIBCO ActiveMatrix Adapter for Database provides a simple means of implementing such interactions.

There are two arguments typically leveled against the use of database triggers: efficiency and the need to modify the database to insert the trigger. Both can be readily addressed.

From the perspective of efficiency, it is almost certainly the case that more work is required to process an individual record when the record is being transmitted via a database trigger than when it is being processed via an ETL exchange. However, the peak resource demand for the trigger approach is liable to be substantially less than for the ETL approach. In other words, you'll need less machine horsepower for the trigger approach. Why? Because the work for the trigger approach will be spread out over time (usually—you'll need to verify this for your case), whereas the ETL exchange happens all at once.

As for modifying the database, many database administrators are loath to add triggers for fear of performance implications. But if you are trying to recognize events, what is the alternative? The alternative is a query that will examine large numbers of records to identify changes. Furthermore, this query will have to be repeated periodically, and the longer the period, the greater the delay in recognizing events. In most situations, the use of the database trigger places less of a burden upon the database.

Many database vendors include the infrastructure for this type of event recognition, using the term Change Data Capture to label these capabilities. An overview of these capabilities can be found on Wikipedia.[1]

Combining API and Database Interactions

Combining API and Database interactions provides an effective means of implementing bi-directional interactions with many systems. The two approaches complement one another: Each is strong in the direction in which the other is weak. The idea is that you use the API approach in the inbound direction and use the database approach in the outbound direction.

There is some synergy in this combination as well. The database approach requires understanding the database schema, which is often proprietary and subject to change. APIs, on the other hand, tend to be publicly supported interfaces. You can reduce the risk of schema dependency by having the trigger only publish the primary key of the record that has changed and then use the publicly supported API to retrieve the remaining information and publish it.

There is, however, a minor drawback to this two-step publication process: There is a time delay between initial publishing of the key and subsequent invocation of the API to retrieve the remaining information. If there is a change to the database during this interval, the API call will return the latest information, not the information that was present at the time the trigger was invoked. Nevertheless, the approach is so powerful that it is actually the design basis for a number of the TIBCO ActiveMatrix adapters to commercial systems.

Direct Interaction via ActiveMatrix-Supported Protocols

Interaction with an external system that uses one of the protocols supported by ActiveMatrix is straightforward. There are two possible

---

1. http://en.wikipedia.org/wiki/Change_data_capture

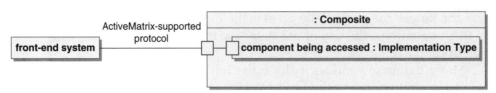

Figure 15-2: *System-Initiated Direct Interaction via ActiveMatrix-Supported Protocol*

patterns, depending upon which party is initiating the interaction. Figure 15-2 shows the architecture pattern when the external system initiates the interaction. This pattern generally arises with front-end systems interacting with users or other systems belonging to customers or business partners. Note that this pattern requires the external system to recognize the triggering event and initiate the interaction.

Figure 15-3 shows the architecture pattern when it is the ActiveMatrix component that recognized the triggering event and initiates the interaction. This pattern generally arises when the external system is either a back-office internal system or an external customer or partner system.

The following protocols can be used with these patterns:

- SOAP over HTTP
- SOAP over JMS
- XML over JMS

Note that SOAP over ActiveMatrix Virtualization cannot be used since that protocol can only be used to communicate with ActiveMatrix-hosted components.

Because these patterns use ActiveMatrix-supported protocols, both the services and references are usable as policy enforcement points for access control policies. Furthermore, the ActiveMatrix framework gathers detailed data about each interaction. This enables both the statistical monitoring of the interactions and the detection of breakdowns.

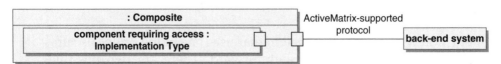

Figure 15-3: *ActiveMatrix-Initiated Direct Interaction via ActiveMatrix-Supported Protocol*

Indirect Interaction via ActiveMatrix Adapters

Although it is convenient to interact with external systems via ActiveMatrix-supported protocols, many external systems do not support such interfaces. However, TIBCO provides a wide range of adapters for interacting with external systems. An adapter is a component that acts as an intermediary between ActiveMatrix and the external system. It interacts with ActiveMatrix with one of the ActiveMatrix-supported protocols and with the external system using one of its native interfaces. As a rule, using adapters takes considerably less effort than writing code to interact with systems.

All TIBCO adapters can be run as stand-alone processes. Some additionally offer the option of running within an ActiveMatrix node. This gives rise to four different architecture patterns. Figure 15-4 shows the available patterns when the external system is the initiator of the interaction. Beyond simple request-response interactions, these patterns are very useful for systems of record to announce information changes.

Figure 15-5 shows the architecture patterns available when the ActiveMatrix component initiates the interaction.

The following adapters can be hosted either stand-alone or within an older TIBCO ActiveMatrix 2.x environment. Most of these adapters will, over time, become available in the 3.x environment.

- TIBCO ActiveMatrix® Adapter for Database
- TIBCO ActiveMatrix® Adapter for Files (Unix/Win)
- TIBCO ActiveMatrix® Adapter for IBM i
- TIBCO ActiveMatrix® Adapter for Kenan BP

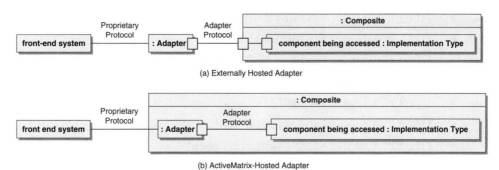

Figure 15-4: *System-Initiated Indirect Interaction via Adapters*

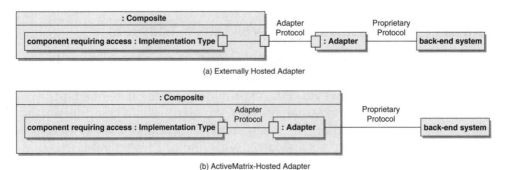

(a) Externally Hosted Adapter

(b) ActiveMatrix-Hosted Adapter

Figure 15-5: *ActiveMatrix-Initiated Indirect Interaction via Adapters*

- TIBCO ActiveMatrix® Adapter for LDAP
- TIBCO ActiveMatrix® Adapter for Lotus Notes
- TIBCO ActiveMatrix® Adapter for PeopleSoft
- TIBCO ActiveMatrix® Adapter for SAP
- TIBCO ActiveMatrix® Adapter for Siebel
- TIBCO ActiveMatrix® Adapter for Tuxedo
- TIBCO ActiveMatrix® Adapter for WebSphere MQ

The following adapters can be only run in the stand-alone mode.

- TIBCO® Adapter for CICS
- TIBCO® Adapter for Clarify
- TIBCO® Adapter for COM
- TIBCO® Adapter for CORBA
- TIBCO® Adapter for EJB
- TIBCO® Adapter for Files i5/OS
- TIBCO® Adapter for Files z/OS
- TIBCO® Adapter for Infranet
- TIBCO® Adapter for JDE OneWorld XE
- TIBCO® Adapter for Remedy
- TIBCO® Adapter for SWIFT
- TIBCO® Adapter for Teradata
- TIBCO® Adapter SDK: Build your own!

It is worth noting that the last adapter, the Adapter SDK, is really not an adapter at all—it is a software development kit for writing your own adapters. What it contains are the class libraries that TIBCO uses to write its own adapters. Using these libraries simplifies the process of implementing the Adapter-to-ActiveMatrix side of the interface and building an adapter that is deployed, monitored, and managed in the same manner as the other TIBCO stand-alone adapters.

Finally, it should be mentioned that other components can play the role of adapter as well. This is appropriate when the mapping between the ActiveMatrix communications and the interactions with the external systems is not one-to-one. TIBCO ActiveMatrix BusinessWorks is often employed in this role.

Direct Interaction via Non-ActiveMatrix-Supported Protocols

The third category of interaction patterns involves direct interaction, but using protocols that are not represented by SCA services and references. Figure 15-6 shows the architecture pattern when the external system initiates the interaction. This is a common pattern when the ActiveMatrix WebApp implementation type is being used and the external system (in this case, a browser) is interacting with the HTTP interface on the WebApp.

Figure 15-7 shows the architecture pattern when the interaction is initiated by the ActiveMatrix component. This is a common pattern when the external system is a database and the ActiveMatrix component is accessing the database via JDBC.

While simple, direct interaction via a non-ActiveMatrix protocol has its limitations. With some notable exceptions (e.g., the HTTP interface on the WebApp implementation type), most of these interfaces cannot be policy enforcement points and no data is collected by ActiveMatrix about the usage of these interfaces.

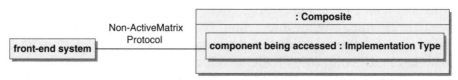

Figure 15-6: *System-Initiated Direct Interaction via Non-ActiveMatrix Protocol*

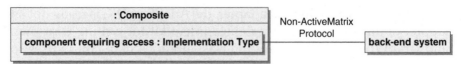

Figure 15-7: *ActiveMatrix-Initiated Direct Interaction via Non-ActiveMatrix Protocol*

General Considerations

Each of the interaction patterns has its strengths and weaknesses, and each has its appropriate applications. Here are a few things to be considered:

- As a rule of thumb, it is good practice to minimize the number of moving parts in a solution. This consideration favors the direct interaction patterns.
- If a single external system requires both types of interaction (system-initiated and ActiveMatrix-initiated), the design and administration will be simpler if the same type of pattern is used in both directions. In many cases, this consideration favors the use of adapters.
- The use of an ActiveMatrix-supported protocol provides both a policy enforcement point and the infrastructure to gather data regarding the use of the interface.

Database Interactions

Interacting with databases is a common requirement. There are two readily available options for this interaction: direct interaction via JDBC and indirect interaction via the Database adapter. Each of these patterns has appropriate usages.

Direct access via JDBC is generally appropriate when the ActiveMatrix component is, in some sense, the "owner" of the database, or at least some of the information in it. When this is the case, interaction only occurs in one direction, with the ActiveMatrix component always initiating the interaction. This strategy is particularly effective when combined with the BusinessWorks implementation type with its readily configured JDBC activities. This option, however, is not appropriate when the ActiveMatrix component needs to be informed of changes to the database arising from other sources.

Indirect access via the Database adapter is generally used when ActiveMatrix components need to be informed of changes to a database. Configuring the adapter places triggers in the database that initiate interactions when database changes occur. However, this strategy does involve the use of an extra component, the adapter, and its interface.

File Interactions

There are two common options for interacting with files: direct interaction with the file system using the BusinessWorks implementation type and the File adapter. Once again, each has its appropriate usages.

Direct interaction with BusinessWorks provides interaction capabilities in both directions. BusinessWorks can detect changes to files (creation and modification) and initiate a wide variety of activities in response. It can also coordinate the creation, updating, renaming, and moving of files with other activities.

The File Adapter provides similar capabilities. In the outbound direction (from the external system), it can detect the creation and modification of files, and optionally rename or move them after they have been processed. In the inbound direction, it can create and append to files, and optionally call a command-line executable to trigger the system's consumption of the file.

There are some differences in capability between BusinessWorks and the File Adapter. Although BusinessWorks generally provides the simpler solution, its parsing capabilities are not as rich as those of the file adapter. It also has limitations when it comes to the size of the file that it can handle, whereas the file adapter can handle arbitrarily large files.

Summary

Interactions with external systems depend upon the interfaces provided by those systems. Four common mechanisms are used for such interactions: application programming interfaces (APIs), databases, files, and protocols.

APIs are useful for interactions that are inbound to the system, but few systems provide callbacks to allow the system to call external code. Many applications have underlying databases, and these provide another mechanism for interaction. Databases tend to be good in the outbound direction, as extracting data from a database is straightforward (provided you know the schema). However, in the inbound direction, it is generally unacceptable to bypass application logic and update the database directly.

Many systems are able to both produce and consume files. For these systems, file-based interactions can be a good mechanism.

A protocol is logically an API tied to a transport, and it has the same limitations. Protocols tend to provide a good mechanism in the inbound direction, and little or no capability in the outbound direction.

One of the biggest challenges in systems' interaction is recognizing events within the system—events that you would like to have trigger an outbound communication. The Adapter for Database provides a convenient mechanism for event recognition, placing triggers in the database that initiate the publication of database changes.

The API and database mechanisms can be effectively combined to provide good system interactions in both directions: Each is strong where the other is weak. This combination provides the architectural basis for a number of TIBCO adapters.

When it comes to interactions between ActiveMatrix components and external systems, there are three primary design patterns:

- Direct interaction via ActiveMatrix-supported protocols, such as SOAP over HTTP or JMS, and XML over JMS
- Indirect interaction via TIBCO adapters
- Direct interaction via non-ActiveMatrix-supported protocols, such as HTTP and JDBC

When it comes to database and file interactions, there are two viable strategies for each. For databases, you can interact with the database directly using JDBC or you can use the database adapter. For files, you can interact with the file system directly or you can use the file adapter. In both cases, the TIBCO ActiveMatrix BusinessWorks implementation type makes direct interactions easy to implement.

Chapter 16

Two-Party Coordination Patterns

Once two parties are talking to one another, typically the next challenge is to coordinate their activities. Coordination defines how the execution of an activity in one component is related to the execution of another activity in another component. How you go about coordinating activities impacts both normal behavior and the ability to detect breakdowns in the process. In terms of breakdown detection, you want to know which party (if any) is in a position to detect the breakdown, and how they know that a breakdown occurred.

This chapter examines a number of design patterns that can be used to coordinate the activities of two parties, and the next chapter explores how these patterns generalize to three or more parties. The patterns discussed in this chapter are:

- Fire-and-Forget
- Request-Reply
- Delegation
- Delegation with Confirmation
- Distributed Transactions
- Third-Party Process Coordinator

Fire-and-Forget Coordination

The simplest possible coordination pattern is fire-and-forget (Figure 16-1). In this pattern, one party simply sends a message to the other, and there is no other communication. Note that either the In-Out or Out-In interaction pattern can be used to implement this coordination.

The advantage of fire-and-forget is that it is simple to implement. Its disadvantage is that neither party is in a position to know whether the interaction succeeded. The sender has no idea whether the recipient received the message or took appropriate action. The recipient has no idea whether a message was sent. Breakdown detection is impossible with this pattern. Improving the communications channel quality of service does not improve the breakdown detection—it only makes a breakdown less likely.

This pattern can be implemented with any of the ActiveMatrix-supported protocols: SOAP In-Only (any transport), and XML over JMS In-Only or Out-Only. File-based interactions also follow this pattern, along with e-mail and any other form of one-way messaging. Many TIBCO Adapter interactions are fire-and-forget as well.

Despite the limitations of this pattern, it is still possible to implement a relatively robust business process with it. Consider the process of paying your bills by mail. You receive your bill via the mail—a one-way communication. You pay your bill via the same one-way service. However, the business process is tolerant of breakdowns. If, for any reason (loss of the bill, your failure to pay, or loss of the payment), your bill does not get paid, the past-due amount is simply added to the next month's bill.

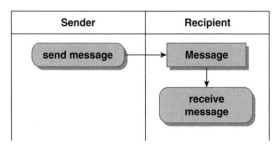

Figure 16-1: *Fire-and-Forget Coordination*

Request-Reply Coordination

In the synchronous variation of request-reply coordination (Figure 16-2), the service consumer sends a request to the service provider and waits for a reply. With this pattern, the receipt of the reply indicates the status of the request: Either the service provider performed the required service or it failed.

There is, however, a third possible outcome in this exchange: the absence of a reply. Without a service-level agreement (SLA) specifying the time frame within which a reply is expected, the absence of a reply is ambiguous with respect to breakdown detection. The service consumer cannot draw any conclusions about the state of the process. With the SLA, however, the situation clarifies: Within the specified time frame, the absence of a reply is acceptable; beyond that time frame, there is a problem. Thus it becomes imperative in any request-reply exchange to establish a response-time SLA for the service provider.

Although the request-reply coordination pattern (with an established response-time SLA) can detect breakdowns, it does not provide sufficient information in all cases to determine the nature of the breakdown. For example, the loss of the request, the failure of the service provider to fulfill the request, or the loss of the reply will all result in the same symptom: the absence of a reply.

The synchronous pattern can be implemented with any of the ActiveMatrix-supported protocols: SOAP In-Out (any transport), and XML over JMS In-Out or Out-In. JDBC interactions follow this pattern, along with HTTP, CORBA, COM, and JRMI interactions. Some TIBCO Adapter interactions are request-reply as well.

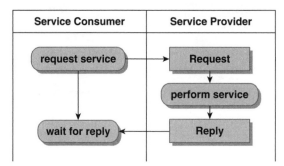

Figure 16-2: *Synchronous Request-Reply Coordination*

Asynchronous variations of this pattern are also possible, but with a limited choice of protocols (see the discussion of the asynchronous variations of the In-Out interaction pattern in Chapter 11). Asynchronous designs are considerably more complicated and tend to be employed only when the time frame for performing the service is long enough to make it impractical for the service consumer to wait for completion.

Delegation

There are situations in which the length of time it takes to perform the service makes it impractical for the service consumer to wait around for a response. Yet, at the same time, you may want to ensure that the service provider got the request and agreed to perform the service. This is the purpose of the delegation pattern (Figure 16-3).

In this pattern the service provider does, indeed, reply to the service consumer, but the reply simply indicates that the request has been received and that the service provider promises to perform the

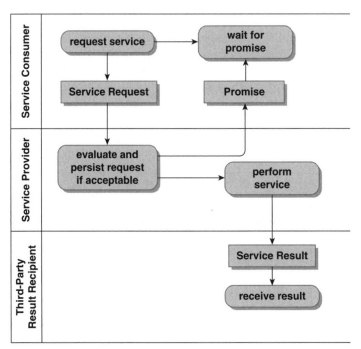

Figure 16-3: *Delegation Pattern*

requested service at some point in the future. Note that this is a bit stronger than a mere acknowledgment that the request was received: Due diligence on the part of the service provider requires that the request be recorded in such a way that the service provider does not lose it. Presumably there is also some obligation to ensure that the pending requests are not ignored either. It is common in this pattern for the actual result to go to a third party rather than back to the service consumer.

This pattern can be viewed as a combination of the request-reply pattern (for receiving the request and returning the promise) and the fire-and-forget pattern (for performing the service and delivering the result). Its breakdown-detection capabilities reflect exactly this. Assuming that there is a response-time service-level agreement governing the return of the promise, the service consumer is in a position to determine whether the service provider has agreed to perform the work. However, no breakdown detection is possible beyond that point.

Delegation with Confirmation

The delegation with confirmation pattern extends delegation to include an eventual asynchronous response to the service consumer (Figure 16-4). The addition of this feedback (assuming that a response-time SLA is in place for this as well) now puts the service consumer in a position to verify whether or not the work was properly performed—but not necessarily to determine whether the result was properly delivered.

There are several variations of this pattern worth describing. The one depicted in Figure 16-4 uses fire-and-forget to deliver the service result. Consequently, the eventual confirmation to the service consumer only indicates that the result was sent—not that it was received. In another variation, the work result is sent back to the service consumer and serves as the confirmation as well. In this case, the service consumer knows with certainty whether the entire process completed successfully. In a third variation, the service result still goes to a third party, but the third-party exchange uses request-reply. Once again, the service consumer now knows with certainty whether the entire process concluded successfully.

One challenge with this pattern is the mechanism for asynchronous delivery of the confirmation to the service consumer. Ideally, this is an

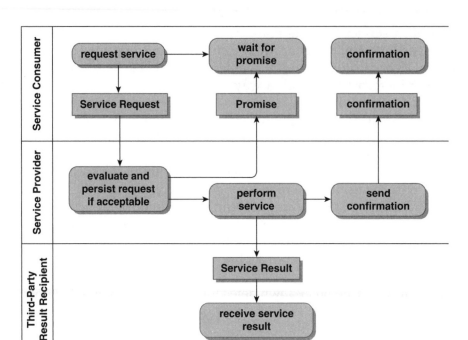

Figure 16-4: *Delegation with Confirmation Pattern*

Out-Only interaction, with the initial request containing the destination to which the confirmation should be sent. This, however, limits the ActiveMatrix transport choice to XML over JMS or requires the use of a non-ActiveMatrix-supported protocol such as e-mail.

Alternatively, the confirmation could be delivered as an In-Only transaction. However, this requires that the service provider be designed to call the specific interface provided by the service consumer. In other words, the service provider is customized for specific service consumers. Some flexibility can be achieved here if all service consumers are required to have the same logical interface (i.e., the same logical WSDL). In such cases a mediation flow with dynamic routing (Figure 14-15) could be used to return the confirmations.

Distributed Transactions

The intent of a transaction is to provide all-or-nothing behavior: Either all participants perform their actions or none of them perform their actions. A transaction requires a manager to govern the execution of the transaction. Depending upon the implementation choices, the manager role may be played by one of the transaction participants or it may be played by a third party. The manager interacts with the participants via some protocol, such as the Open Group's XA standard.[1]

Two-Phase Commit

The standard approach to implementing distributed transactions is to use a two-phase commit protocol (Figure 16-5), with the XA standard being one of the leading examples. A transaction begins with an application program (using XA terminology) initiating the transaction. In the example, the First Party is playing the role of the application program. At this point the transaction manager issues an identifier for the transaction, which is carried through all subsequent interactions related to the transaction. The various parties involved in the transaction (XA resource managers) are each directed to perform their operations by the application program, and each registers with the transaction manager. Note that in this example the First Party is also playing the role of a resource manager. Resource managers do not make the results of their work visible at this time.

When all of the operations have been completed, the application program tells the transaction manager to commit the transaction. The transaction manager now interacts with the transaction participants (XA resource managers) in two phases. In the first phase, each party is asked to vote on whether the transaction should be committed. Assuming all parties vote yes, each party is then asked to make their changes permanent and visible. If anyone votes no, all parties are asked to roll back the transaction.

It is not a simple matter for a party to be a participant (resource manager) in the XA protocol. Each participant must be able to logically do the work without making the results either visible or permanent. When the party votes yes, it is obligated to make a stable (i.e., persistent) record of the information it needs to eventually commit, again without making the results visible.

The consequence of this complexity is that there are, in reality, few systems capable of participating in two-phase commit transactions,

---

1. The Open Group, *Distributed TP: The XA Specification*, www.opengroup.org/bookstore/catalog/c193.htm.

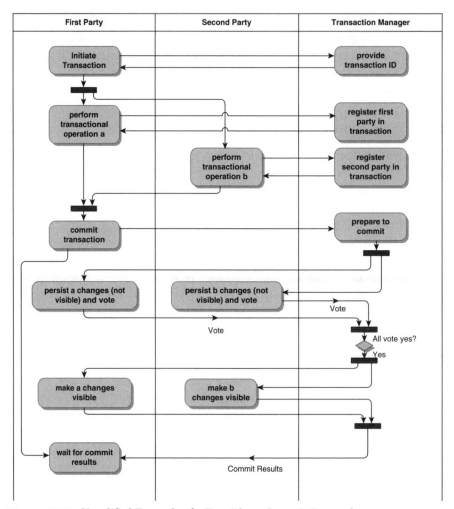

Figure 16-5: *Simplified Example of a Two-Phase Commit Protocol*

with databases being the most common. This, in itself, limits the usability of the two-phase commit protocol. At the time of this writing, composites of interacting ActiveMatrix components can only be grouped into a transaction if they are deployed in the same node.

In the meantime, this does not prevent an individual component from playing the role of the application program and possibly that of a resource manager as well. TIBCO ActiveMatrix BusinessWorks is well suited for this role. It includes an XA transaction manager and a number of activities (including JDBC database interactions, and the sending and receiving of JMS messages) that can be transaction participants.

This allows BusinessWorks to play the roles of application, resource manager, and transaction manager. It can also work with an external XA transaction manager.

Messaging and Transactions

The coordination of message sending and receipt within a transaction requires careful consideration. Sending a message in a nontransactional manner will not recall that message in the event of a transaction roll-back. Similarly, receiving a message in a nontransactional manner will consume the message even if the transaction is rolled back. TIBCO ActiveMatrix BusinessWorks allows you to send and receive messages as part of the transaction. For message sending, the message is given to the EMS server but not released for delivery until the transaction commits. A transaction rollback or failure (such as the restart of the BW engine in the middle of the transaction) will result in the message being deleted without being delivered. For message receipt, the acknowledgment of message receipt is not given to the EMS server until the transaction commits. A transaction rollback or failure will result in the message being re-delivered to the next eligible recipient.

As things stand today, when messaging is involved, the scope of the transaction boundary does not extend beyond the messaging server. In particular, the activities of the party receiving a message sent as part of a transaction are not within the scope of the transaction. Thus, your design must take this into consideration. It is worth noting that the TIBCO ActiveMatrix Policy Framework (discussed in Chapter 13) and emerging public standards such as WS-AtomicTransaction are beginning to lay the foundation for extending transactions in this manner, but under most circumstances such transactions are not practical today.

Distributed Transaction Limitations

The all-or-nothing behavior of transactions has some limitations as well:

- All parties must be up and running for the transaction (and thus the business process) to proceed. If any of the parties is unavailable (system down, network problems, etc.), nothing happens. For many business processes, this is not the desired behavior.
- The protocol does not address what to do if the transaction fails: The transaction manager simply informs the application program

of the failure. It is then up to the application program to figure out what to do next.

- Resources involved in the transaction are locked for the duration of the transaction. This limits the usability to short-lived transactions.

Third-Party Process Coordinator

In a two-phase commit transaction, the application program (XA terminology) initiates the transaction, initiates the execution of the transaction operations (directly or indirectly), commits the transaction, and has to deal with the consequences of a failed transaction. It is, in effect, orchestrating the activities of the transaction participants and coordinating the performance of their work. However, the role of process coordinator (Figure 16-6) does not necessarily require the use of a two-phase commit transaction. The process coordinator can use any of the coordination techniques described here to orchestrate the activities of the business process participants.

Because the process coordinator is not constrained to use any particular coordination technique, it can apply whichever techniques are appropriate for the situation. This can include the use of compensating transactions (discussed in the next section) and even the implementation of alternate business processes when the primary business process is unable to execute normally.

The role of the process coordinator in a business process is as important as that of any of the participants. Thus, it is essential that the participant playing this role be made clear when defining the solution architecture. The process coordinator must, at a minimum, appear in the architecture pattern and in the mapping of the process onto that pattern. It is not uncommon for the activities of the process coordinator to show up in the process model as well.

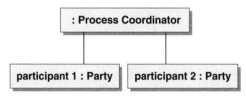

Figure 16-6: *Process Coordinator*

TIBCO has three products that are designed to play the process coordinator role. TIBCO ActiveMatrix BusinessWorks provides a straightforward means of implementing short-running automated processes. TIBCO ActiveMatrix BPM provides the capability of managing longer-running and more complex processes typically involving people as well as systems. TIBCO BusinessEvents provides the ability to implement processes that are so complex that they can only be effectively characterized by a set of rules.

Compensating Transactions

A powerful and useful alternative to the two-phase commit transaction is the compensating transaction. A compensating transaction reverses the net effect of a previous operation without modifying the previous operation. For example, when you return a purchase for credit, the initial sales transaction is not deleted or modified. Instead, a second transaction credits your account with the equivalent amount. The credit is a compensating transaction.

Approximating a Two-Phase Commit with Compensating Transactions

Compensating transactions, when used by a process coordinator, provide a means of approximating the behavior of a two-phase commit transaction (Figure 16-7). The process coordinator asks each of the participants to perform its required activity. Note that these activities are actually performed and the results are immediately visible. If all of the activities succeed (and you need to use appropriate coordination patterns to ensure that breakdowns can be detected), then the work is done. However, if any of the parties fails to perform its activity, the process coordinator then tells the other participants (those that reported success) to perform their compensating transactions. This effectively gives you the rollback of the two-phase commit.

Compensating Transaction Strengths and Limitations

Compensating transactions have the advantage that they impose virtually no overhead when the transaction completes successfully. Extra work is done only in the event that one of the parties fails to succeed in

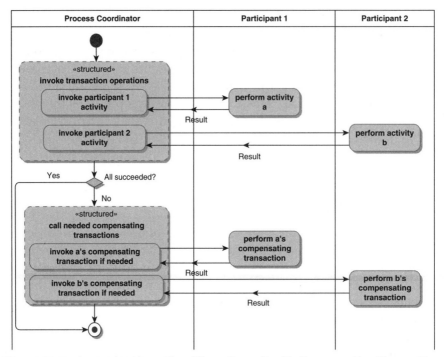

Figure 16-7: *Approximating a Two-Phase Commit with Compensating Transactions*

performing its assigned task. In contrast, every two-phase commit transaction adds overhead whether or not it succeeds.

Compensating transactions also have a significant limitation: Some activities do not have compensating transactions. Once you print a page, it is hard to get the ink back off the paper. Nevertheless, it is still possible to approximate a two-phase commit transaction if there is only one activity that does not have a compensating transaction (Figure 16-8). The trick is to leave the activity without the compensating transaction until last. If all the other activities succeed, then you attempt the activity without the compensating transaction. If it succeeds, you are done. If it fails, then you perform the compensating transactions for the other activities.

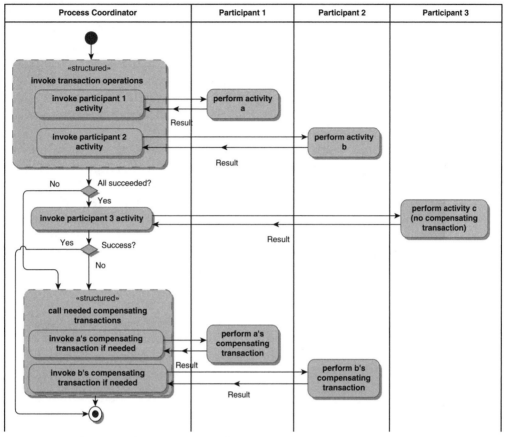

Figure 16-8: *Coping with an Activity without a Compensating Transaction*

Summary

Coordination defines how the execution of an activity is related to the execution of other activities. There are a number of patterns that can be used for this purpose. These patterns differ in their ability to detect breakdowns in the process.

Fire-and-Forget is the simplest form of coordination, but it is incapable of detecting any form of breakdown. Request-reply can detect breakdowns, but unambiguously interpreting the absence of a reply requires a response-time service-level agreement (SLA).

Delegation uses request-reply to return a promise to perform the service at some later point in time, and it uses fire-and-forget for the remainder of the process. It can detect breakdowns in making the promise, but not in the subsequent performance of the work. Delegation with Confirmation adds an eventual asynchronous confirmation that the work was completed. It extends breakdown detection to the entire process, providing that appropriate coordination patterns are used for intermediate interactions.

Distributed transactions formalize the dialog between parties required to achieve all-or-nothing behavior: Either all parties succeed in their work, or no work is performed. However, they provide no mechanism for describing what should happen if the transaction fails. Adding a Process Coordinator to the picture provides a home for additional coordination logic, which can employ compensating transactions to approximate the behavior of a distributed transaction. Some activities do not have compensating transactions. Nevertheless, one of these activities can be incorporated into an approximated distributed transaction by leaving it to last.

Chapter 17

Multi-Party Coordination Patterns

The two-party coordination patterns of the previous chapter generalize to situations involving three or more parties. This chapter explores four of these generalizations and offers some thoughts on data validation and breakdown detection in multi-party situations. The patterns discussed in this chapter include:

- Multi-Party Fire-and-Forget
- Multi-Party Request-Reply
- Multi-Party Delegation with Confirmation

The three other coordination patterns from the previous chapter, Delegation, Distributed Transactions, and Third-Party Process Coordinator, also extend to multiple parties. However, the discussion of these patterns in the previous chapter, augmented with the additional discussion in this chapter, is sufficient to cover their multi-party extensions. Therefore, these patterns will not be discussed further in this chapter.

Multi-Party Fire-and-Forget

The Multi-Party Fire-and-Forget pattern (Figure 17-1) is pretty much what you would expect. The pattern generally arises when the service provider sends its service result to a third party. Commonly, the arrival of the service result also serves as a trigger (an implicit request) for the third party to perform some work.

As with its two-party cousin, the Multi-Party Fire-and-Forget pattern is simple (and therefore inexpensive) to implement, but it offers no breakdown detection anywhere in the process.

Multi-Party Request-Reply

The multi-party extension to synchronous request-reply is shown in Figure 17-2. This extension, like its two-party cousin, is very robust with respect to breakdown detection—again, with the caveat concerning the need for response-time service-level agreements. The pattern

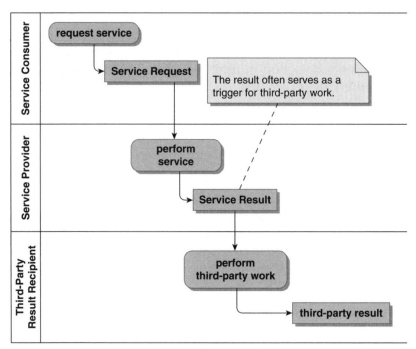

Figure 17-1: *Multi-Party Fire-and-Forget*

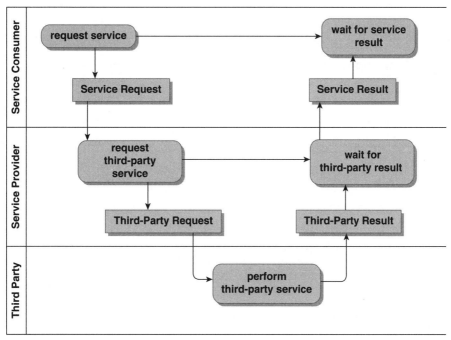

Figure 17-2: *Synchronous Multi-Party Request Reply*

also tends to extend the length of time that the service consumer waits for the reply since latency is added in each layer of the exchange. Furthermore, resources are tied up for every participant waiting for the reply. When the request volume is high, and/or the nesting is deep, the resulting resource consumption can be a significant factor in the design and should be carefully considered.

Multi-Party Delegation with Confirmation

Just as the two-party delegation with confirmation pattern had several variants, so does the multi-party pattern. Figure 17-3 shows a variation in which the hand-off to the third party is treated as part of providing the service, and the eventual hand-off of the third-party result is accomplished via fire-and-forget.

With the exception of the delivery of the third-party result, this pattern can detect any breakdown in the process. Breakdown detection could be further strengthened by delivering the third-party result via request reply or some other breakdown-detecting pattern.

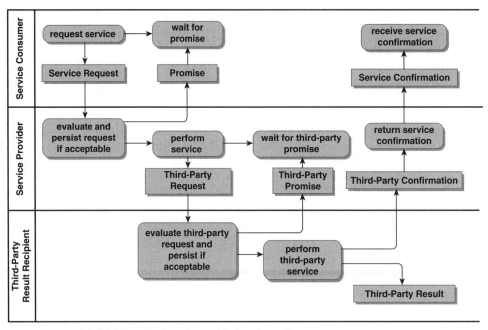

Figure 17-3: *Multi-Party Delegation with Confirmation*

The major advantage of this pattern over the multi-party request-reply is that the resources of the service consumer and intermediate parties are not tied up during the time it takes to perform the work. The disadvantage is that the eventual confirmations are delivered asynchronously, resulting in a more complex design (see the discussion of the two-party request-reply pattern in the previous chapter).

Data Validation

A common requirement in a distributed solution is that the validity of information must be checked at some point in the process. Such requirements give rise to two questions: What kind of validation is required? And where should this validation occur?

Types of Validation

Validation can run the gamut from simple syntactic checks through complex analysis of the data. Some of the most common techniques are the following:

- Syntactic validation: Checking the format of the supplied information. With XML the process involves validating the XML against its defining schema.
- Self-consistency checks: Comparing data elements against one another for logical consistency. For example, is the requested delivery date on an order on or after the order placement date?
- External reference checks: Determining whether the data correspond to information saved in some system. Does the supplied customerID match one in the customer database?

Where to Validate Impacts Coordination Pattern Selection

Looking at the example in Figure 17-4, there are multiple points within this process at which the information in the initial service request might be validated. The design question is: Where is the optimal place for validation?

A good rule of thumb is to perform validation as close to the origin of the information as possible. This is because correcting the information is generally easier the closer you are to the source. Based on this

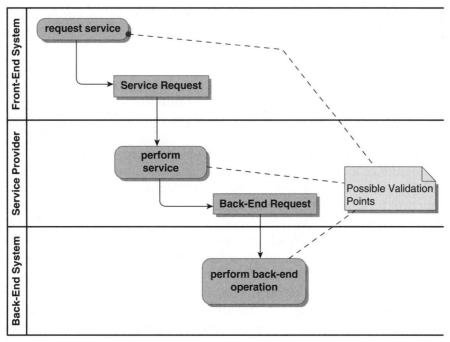

Figure 17-4: *Possible Points of Validation in a Front-to-Back Dialog*

guideline, the ideal place to validate in the Figure 17-4 example would be in the front-end system itself, which is likely a user interface. There, errors can be detected and the user immediately prompted to correct the error.

Second best would be to have the service provider validate the information in the incoming service request. However, a problem immediately arises: Since this is a fire-and-forget interaction, there is no mechanism available to correct invalid inputs. If you want to fix a problem here, you need to design a secondary process by which the invalid input is identified, corrected, and resubmitted. This recovery process can be as complicated as the mainstream process!

Another alternative would be to replace the Fire-and-Forget interaction with a Request-Reply or Delegation pattern. This would afford the opportunity for the front-end system to prompt the user to correct the invalid information. Although not as simple as catching the error initially, it is simpler than designing a secondary process.

An aside regarding the use of SOAP faults is in order here. Rule of thumb: If you are designing for the exception, don't use a SOAP fault to return it. Instead, design the return data structure to represent both the normally expected data and the alternative results that can arise. The reason is that handling SOAP faults generally breaks the process flow in the component receiving the faults. This makes it very complicated for that component to recover by taking some action and then resuming the process.

Similar considerations apply to placing the validation in the back-end system. Fire-and-forget would again require a secondary process for recovery, while replacing it with a Multi-Party Request-Reply or Multi-Party Delegation pattern makes it possible for the front-end system to correct the original inputs.

The decision about where to validate also depends somewhat on the nature of the validation being performed. Syntactic validation and self-consistency checks can typically be performed anywhere. It is good practice, for example, to always validate an XML structure—whether the component is creating it or receiving it.

External reference checks, on the other hand, require access to the external data. In the example, if the back-end system is the owner of the data, then this validation can be readily performed in the back-end system. If you wanted to perform that check in either the service or the front-end system, the back-end system would have to provide another interface to access the data (or, alternatively, perform the actual validation).

For this reason, when the business process calls for external reference checks, it is good practice to explicitly model them both in the process model and, most importantly, in the mapping of that model onto the architecture pattern.

Multi-Party Breakdown Detection

The choice of coordination patterns has a direct impact on the solution's ability to detect breakdowns in the business process. Bottom line: If it can't be detected, you can't do anything about it!

The Fire-and-Forget pattern provides no opportunity to detect breakdowns. Request-Reply provides two forms of breakdown detection: a reply that explicitly indicates the existence of a problem and the absence of a reply after the response time SLA has expired. Delegation can detect breakdowns in the work hand-off, but not in the subsequent execution of the service. Adding Confirmation enables the detection of work performance breakdowns. Depending upon the coordination patterns used, it may also be able to detect problems in the delivery of the work result.

Distributed transactions can detect breakdowns in the execution of the transaction, but nothing else. A Process Coordinator can detect problems anywhere in the process provided that it, in turn, uses appropriate coordination patterns when interacting with the process participants.

Adding Feedback to Improve Breakdown Detection

The addition of feedback in a process can greatly improve breakdown detection. Consider the process shown in Figure 17-5. This is essentially a Multi-Party Fire-and-Forget pattern with one addition: The last participant in the process is sending a confirmation back to the first participant confirming that the work was performed. This immediately places the first participant in a position to detect a breakdown anywhere in the process (with the possible exception of the third-party work result delivery, depending upon the coordination used for that).

The implication here is that you can greatly improve the breakdown detection of any process with the selective addition of feedback.

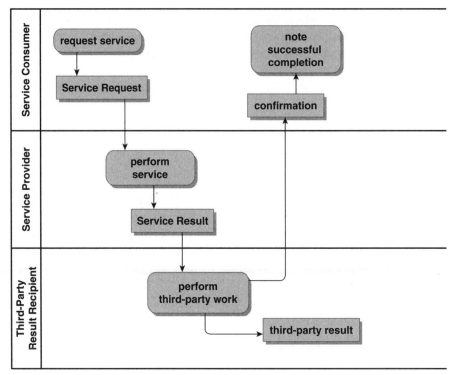

Figure 17-5: *Adding Feedback to Improve Breakdown Detection*

Third-Party Process Monitoring

Another approach to detecting breakdowns is to add a process monitor (Figure 17-6). The monitor captures events that are generated at various points in the process and uses them to determine whether or not

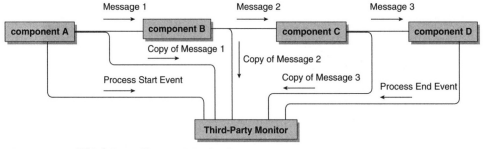

Figure 17-6: *Third-Party Process Monitoring*

the process is executing properly. TIBCO BusinessEvents is ideally suited to play this monitoring role.

Evaluating an Architecture for Breakdown Detection

If you have mapped the business process onto the architecture pattern in the manner described, evaluating the architecture for breakdown detection is a straightforward process. For each participant (swimlane), ask yourself: What would the impact be if that participant failed? Which other participant (if any) would notice, and what would the symptoms be? Then ask the same question for each interaction: What would the impact be? Which participants (if any) would notice and what would the symptoms be?

When you perform this analysis, you will observe an interesting phenomenon: Many different failures typically result in a small number of symptoms. Looking at Figure 17-5, the loss of the Service Provider, Third-Party Recipient, Service Request, Service Result, or Confirmation will all result in the same symptom—the Confirmation will not be received by the Service Consumer. This puts the Service Consumer in a position to detect breakdowns anywhere in the process, although it does not provide sufficient information to determine the nature of the problem.

Finally, you should consider what the component detecting the breakdown should do with the information. You most likely will want this information in a log file, but nobody will know that the error has occurred. It is good practice to annunciate the existence of the breakdown so that at least someone is aware that there is a problem. Doing this requires an understanding of your organization's operations group and the mechanisms available to inform it of problems.

Summary

The two-party coordination patterns extend in consistent ways to multi-party interactions. The Multi-Party Fire-and-Forget pattern is simple, but again affords no opportunity for breakdown detection. Multi-Party Request-Reply can detect all breakdowns, but long response times and high request volumes can tie up many resources. Multi-Party Delegation with Confirmation does not tie up resources while work is being performed but still provides the same level of breakdown detection as Multi-Party Request-Reply.

Data validation is an important consideration in distributed design. There are different types of validation that may be required, including syntactic checks, self-consistency checks, and external reference checks. The location of the data validation impacts the ease with which the process can be recovered from a failed validation. The choice of coordination patterns impacts the ease of recovery.

Breakdown detection is another important consideration that is also impacted by the selection of coordination patterns. Adding feedback to a process can greatly improve breakdown detection. Architectures are readily evaluated for breakdown detection by considering the loss of individual process participants and communications and then determining which remaining participants (if any) are in a position to detect that the process has failed.

Part IV

Building Solutions

Chapter 18

Services

Services and service-oriented architectures are broad and much-discussed topics. This chapter touches on some of the highlights, looking at the concept of a service and why services cost more than traditional implementations. Given that an investment is required to create services, it explores the conditions under which services make sense and provide a return on that investment.

Traditional Approach

A service is a reusable unit of functionality with a standardized (abstracted) interface. Without services, as seen in Figure 18-1(a), a component wishing to use some functionality is tied to the provider of that functionality in a variety of ways. It is tied to the technology of the provider. If the function is a COBOL mainframe transaction, then the using component needs to know how to invoke a COBOL mainframe transaction. If the function is a piece of Java code, then the using component needs to know how to invoke that.

Beyond the technology dependency, a traditional using component needs to understand the semantics of the data structures required to use the native interface. For example, if the component is using the BAPI interface of SAP, the designer had better understand the structure and organization of IDOC data structures.

There are similar ties to native operation semantics as well. For example, placing an order in SAP using the BAPI interface requires two

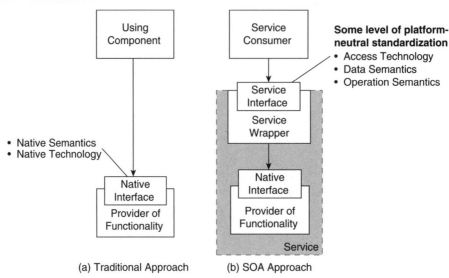

Figure 18-1: *Contrasting Traditional and Service Approaches*

operations: The first takes the order and places it in a staging table; the second retrieves the result from another table. Furthermore, you need to wait some time after calling the first operation before you can expect to find the results with the second operation.

Service-Oriented Architecture (SOA) Approach

Services bring some level of standardization to this interface. Almost always you want to standardize the access technology so that whether the service provider is running on a mainframe, a Unix box, a Windows box, or some other platform, you are able to access the interface from whatever platform the service consumer happens to be running on. Platform neutrality is achieved through the use of platform-agnostic standards, and the platform-specific implementations of those standards are usually acquired.

Beyond standardizing the access technology, you may or may not want to standardize the data semantics and operation semantics. In contrast to the access technology, which you generally acquire, standardized data structures and operations (with some exceptions) generally need to be engineered and implemented. This requires investment, and consequently each service requires an investment decision as to whether the cost of standardizing the data and operation semantics is warranted. And it is perfectly appropriate for the decision to be different for different services.

Standardized Data Semantics: Common Data Models

The argument concerning the standardization of data semantics is really the decision as to whether a common data model should be created for the information being exchanged between the service consumer and the service provider. The argument usually boils down to determining how many parties will use the resulting data model. If there are only two parties involved (one service consumer and one service provider), there is usually little benefit in designing a data structure that is foreign to both parties. On the other hand, if there are three or more parties involved, a well-engineered data structure can go a long way towards simplifying the exchange of information between the parties.

Standardized Operation Semantics

Standardizing operation semantics means defining operations that make sense to both the provider and consumer of the service. Using the earlier SAP example, from a service consumer perspective it might make sense to define a single operation for placing an order, hiding the underlying pair of interactions with SAP.

However, standardizing operation semantics, like standardizing data semantics, requires engineering effort. If there are only two parties involved, it may be difficult to justify the investment. However, when three or more parties are involved, the investment is frequently justifiable.

Benefits of Services

If you look into the volume of literature surrounding SOA and services, you will encounter four commonly cited benefits:

- Platform neutrality: Regardless of the platform upon which the service consumer and service provider reside, they can interoperate.

- Isolation: The service consumer and service provider implementations are separated by the service interface. This isolation allows each to evolve independently, shrinking the scope (and hence the cost) of projects requiring change.

- Reuse: For each new service consumer, rather than building a new interface to the service functionality, the existing service operations can be used. This avoids development work, lowering cost and shortening schedules.

- Flexibility: Services can be combined in new and unique ways to create new business processes. This is really an extension of reuse, with the expected benefit primarily being a reduction in the amount of time it takes to implement the new process.

Most SOA Benefits Require Service Interface Stability

It is significant that three of the four commonly cited SOA benefits stem from one single property: interface stability. Isolation, reuse, and flexibility all assume that the service interface does not change, or at least does not change very often.

This observation is important because you do not get interface stability for free. The level of stability you obtain reflects the level of effort you put into the analysis of how the service will be used.

Interface stability is a relative thing. You will never obtain the perfect service: You can't afford either the time or the effort required to strive for perfection. The good news is that you don't need perfection—you just need interfaces that change more slowly than the implementations on either side of them.

Having said this, you must plan for the changing of interfaces. In a practical sense, this means that you need the ability to deploy two or more versions of the same interface simultaneously. This will afford service consumers the flexibility to migrate to the new version over some period of time. The alternative, a "big bang" simultaneous upgrade of the service and its consumers, is an expensive and risky proposition that is to be assiduously avoided.

Where Do Services Make Sense?

Building a service requires investment. Time and effort must be put into crafting an interface that will remain relatively stable over time. Documentation must be prepared to help first-time users understand what the service is for and how to use it. Mechanisms must be in place for finding appropriate services. Higher levels of testing will be required, since more components will depend on the service. All of these things take time and effort.

For the purpose of this discussion, the point-to-point interfaces that happen to use the technologies providing platform neutrality but do not strive for interface stability will not be considered services. A common example of a non-service is the use of a JMS transport to move an application-specific data structure between a pair of applications.

Recognizing that building a service requires investment raises the question as to when such an investment is warranted, that is, when there will be a return on the investment. Two sets of circumstances are indicators of a return. The first arises when there are two or more different consumers of the service's functionality (Figure 18-2). Here the return on the service investment stems from avoiding the need to build additional interfaces for the additional clients. Instead, the existing service interface is reused. This situation often arises in practice with the addition of new channels for reaching customers and business partners.

The other pattern providing a return on the investment is one in which there are two or more providers of essentially the same functionality (Figure 18-3). This situation frequently arises as a result of mergers and acquisitions. The payback here is to hide from the client the logic needed to determine which of the service providers to use in a given situation. This allows this logic to evolve (as information and responsibility is migrated from one provider to the other) without impacting the client.

Combining these two patterns, the general pattern providing a service return on investment (ROI) is shown in Figure 18-4. When you are counting clients and providers, be sure to take future plans into consideration. It may be that today you only have one client and one provider. However, in the near future you may be planning to add a new client

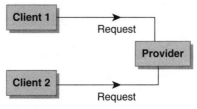

Figure 18-2: *Multiple Service Clients*

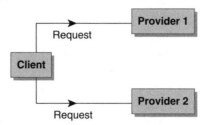

Figure 18-3: *Multiple Service Providers*

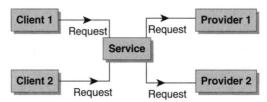

Figure 18-4: *General Pattern Providing Service ROI*

(new channel), or you may be planning to replace the present provider with another. Also count a significant modification as a new system. These situations also warrant the investment in developing the service.

Service Granularity

The granularity of the service—the amount of work encapsulated by each service operation—is an important consideration when conceptualizing a service. Remember that a service generally runs in another operating system process, and potentially on another machine. This means that there is some overhead involved in invoking the service. Therefore, you want to ensure that this overhead is relatively small compared to the work being performed by the service. For example, it would not make sense to abstract arithmetic operations (addition, subtraction, multiplication, and division) into a service: The overhead of invoking each operation would vastly exceed the computational cost of performing the operation.

On the other hand, the more functionality encapsulated into a service, the more specialized the service operations become. Highly specialized operations are less likely to be reusable. So, in conceptualizing your services you want to strike a balance—large enough so that the overhead can be ignored, small enough that it can be reused.

Summary

Services bring some level of abstraction to the interface between a service consumer and a service provider. Almost always, this means standardizing the technology of the interaction so that the service consumer and service provider can communicate regardless of the platform on which each is running. The technologies to accomplish this are generally acquired by the enterprise.

In addition, you may want to standardize the data and operation semantics. Unlike the acquired standardization of the access technology, standardizing data and operation semantics generally requires engineering effort on the part of the enterprise. In other words, an investment must be made.

There are four common benefits attributed to service-oriented architectures: platform neutrality, isolation of service consumer and provider, reuse of services, and the flexibility to build new business processes from existing services. Isolation, reuse, and flexibility all depend on the relative stability of service interfaces.

Achieving interface stability requires an investment in their conceptualization. A return on this investment is realized when the interface is reused or when there are multiple service providers. The granularity of service operations needs to be considered as well. If the work being performed is minimal, the overhead of invoking the service is not warranted. If a lot of work is encapsulated in the operation, it tends to become very specialized and therefore unlikely to be reused.

Chapter 19

Solutions

A solution provides the means of satisfying business requirements and providing value to the enterprise. This book, as a whole, focuses on the architecture of solutions, and this chapter addresses application of the material that has been covered to the architecture of solutions.

To facilitate the discussion, we will employ two examples. One will be the query of a book database based on the query reference architecture discussed in Chapter 4. This example is simple enough that it requires little explanation. The other is a service to validate an individual's membership in a health care plan on a given date. This example is considerably more complicated and requires some explanation.

Solution Architecture

A solution architecture lays out the structure and organization of the solution. Its primary elements are those of any architecture: process models, an architecture pattern, and mappings of the process models onto the architecture pattern.

The solution architecture identifies the business processes impacted by the project and defines their structure in the solution. It identifies the participants (both people and systems) and, by means of the architecture pattern, defines how they will be organized and will communicate with one another. Finally, the solution architecture defines how the business processes map onto the participants in the architecture pattern, detailing the roles and responsibilities of the participants.

At this point, let's take a look at a solution architecture for one of our examples, the Membership Validation Service.

Membership Validation Service

Membership Validation Service Requirements

In the health care arena, there are occasions when it is necessary to determine whether a given individual is covered by a particular health plan as of a given date. This may occur during the processing of a health care claim or when a health care provider, prior to performing a service, needs to determine whether an individual is presently covered.

The membership validation service will be provided by Nouveau Health Care, an enterprise that is both a health plan issuer (i.e., an insurance company) and an administrative processing house for other health plan issuers.

The service will be made available to a number of parties: claims processors within the enterprise, claims processors external to the enterprise, and health care providers. Internal access will be provided via SOAP with a JMS transport, and external access via SOAP with an HTTP transport. Parties using the service must provide credentials and be authenticated and authorized. The service must support multiple types of credentials including userid/password pairs and digital certificates.

The membership validation service provides a single operation at its interface (Figure 19-1). Input to this operation comprises identifying information about the health care plan issuer, the plan itself, the member whose membership is being checked, and the date of service for which validation of coverage is being requested. The operation responds by indicating whether the member identifier has been found associated with the indicated health plan and whether the membership in the plan was valid on the date specified.

The service is intended to be a wrapper around existing capabilities for validating membership. Consequently, the service must be capable of interacting with a number of back-end systems. Some of these systems are local to the Nouveau Health Care. Others belong to third-party business partners for which the Nouveau serves as an administrative processing center.

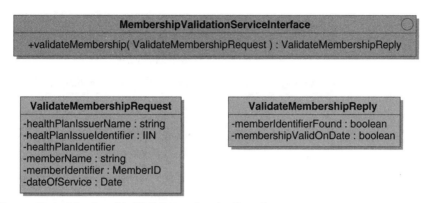

Figure 19-1: *Membership Validation Service Interface*

The local systems are databases that will be accessed via JDBC. There are several such systems, each supporting a different set of health plans. One of these external systems has already been identified and will be accessed via a SOAP over HTTP interface. Others are, at this time, unidentified, but provisions must be made for their incorporation at some future point. Although the details of the future interfaces have not been defined, it should be assumed that the information content of the `ValidateMembershipRequest` is sufficient to support the interaction. Access to all back-end systems will require credentials for authentication and authorization. Credentials will either be userid/passwords or digital certificates.

Membership Validation Solution Architecture

In the membership validation example, there is a single business process: Validate Membership (Figure 19-2). The process is very straightforward. It takes in the information for the query and, using a cross-reference table maintained by the service, determines the back-end system to which the request should be directed. It then reformats the request as required by the back-end system, submits the back-end query, and obtains the answer. The answer is then converted into the format specified by the service and returned.

Note that the process also indicates what should happen if exceptions arise. This defines the business process response to problems. In this example, the business process response is to simply announce that something went wrong. However, in many business processes there are alternate courses of action that are expected to be pursued when

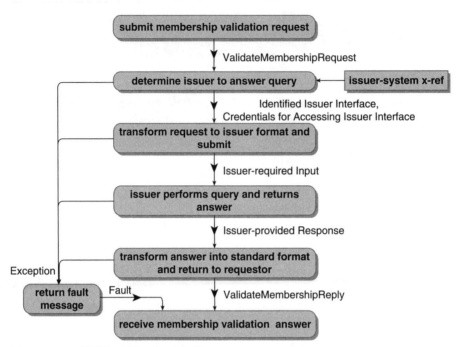

Figure 19-2: *Validate Membership Process*

specific problems arise. It is important to capture these as part of the process definition.

The architecture pattern for the service is shown in Figure 19-3. The service consumers will interact with the service using SOAP with either JMS or HTTP as the transport. The service interacts with back-end systems in a variety of ways. The local systems are databases that will be accessed via JDBC. The partner system that has been defined at this point has a SOAP interface that utilizes HTTP as a transport. Other partner systems have yet to be defined, but the service architecture should be designed in such a way as to readily accommodate new back-end interactions.

The mapping of the process onto the architecture pattern is shown in Figure 19-4. There are three significant design decisions that were made in defining this mapping. One is that the entire interaction from service consumer to issuer system and back will follow the Multi-Party Request Reply pattern described in Chapter 17. The second is that the issuer-system cross-reference will be part of the Membership Validation Service. The third is that any exception raised within the service will result in the return of a SOAP fault.

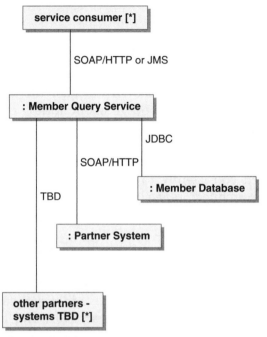

Figure 19-3: *Membership Validation Architecture Pattern*

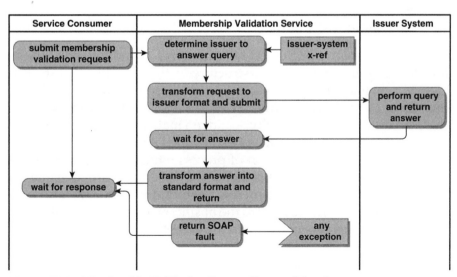

Figure 19-4: *Membership Validation Process-Pattern Mapping*

Refinement

The solution architecture, of course, is not a complete solution. Much detail has to be added in order to obtain a working solution. But, at the same time, adding the detail should not alter the architecture. This raises the question as to how you go about adding detail and, at the same time, ensure that you are not altering the architecture. The answer is by using the process of refinement.

Refinement means adding detail without altering structure. This concept, applied consistently to the three architecture perspectives, ensures that the architecture itself is not altered. This, in turn, ensures that any reasoning and analysis that were applied to the architecture are still valid for the completed solution.

In reality, it is not always possible to complete the implementation of a solution through refinement. Issues can arise during implementation that were not considered in the architecture and require a modification of the architecture in order to address them. When these situations arise, raise the issue to the architect and let the architect determine the appropriate modification to the architecture. It is important to do this because the modifications may have consequences that cannot be anticipated without the full architectural perspective.

Process Model Refinement

Refining a process model adds internal detail to individual activities but does not alter the original structure of the activities. Figure 19-5 shows an architectural process model and a proper refinement from the implementation. Internal structure has been added to activity B, but this activity still follows activity A and, no matter what internal path is taken within the activity, is succeeded by activity C.

The most common violation of process refinement typically arises as a result of exceptions whose handling was not specified as part of the process model. At this point, it is important to re-engage the architect (who may, in turn, go back to the business) to determine the appropriate business process response to the exception.

Architecture Pattern Refinement

Refining the architecture pattern adds internal detail to the elements of the architecture pattern without altering the original structure. Figure 19-6 takes another look at the ATM example discussed back in Chapter 3. It

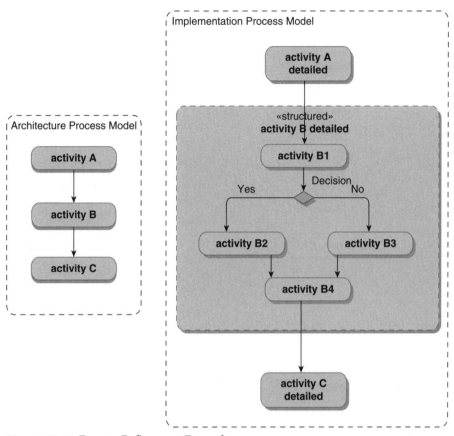

Figure 19-5: *Process Refinement Example*

supposes that the original architecture specification indicated only that there would be an ATM system and left the internal structure of that system unspecified. The refinement, used in the implementation, indicates that the ATM system comprises two types of components: ATM Machines and an ATM Server. ATM Machines interact with the ATM Server which, in turn, interacts with the Bank Servers.

Architecture pattern refinement precludes adding components that are not sub-components of existing elements. You cannot, for example, add other systems as users of the ATM system—this would be an architectural change. Similarly, you cannot add another communications channel, such as a Bluetooth connection between the Person's cell phone and the ATM system. This, too, would be an architecture change.

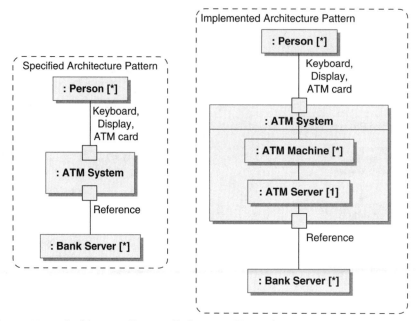

Figure 19-6: *Architecture Pattern Refinement Example*

Mapping Refinement

As we noted back in Chapter 3, many design decisions are made in the process of creating the mapping between the process model and the architecture pattern. For this reason, it is important to apply the concept of refinement here as well so that the reasoning behind these design decisions remains valid.

Figure 19-7 shows the mapping for the ATM example at an early stage in the architecture in which the ATM system has no sub-structure.

Figure 19-8 shows the mapping after the ATM System structure has been refined to incorporate the sub-structure of ATM Machines and an ATM Server. Note that although some of the original ATM System activities have just been assigned to either the ATM Machine or ATM Server, others have been decomposed. This decomposition requires interaction among the sub-activities, and thus communications between the ATM Machine and ATM server.

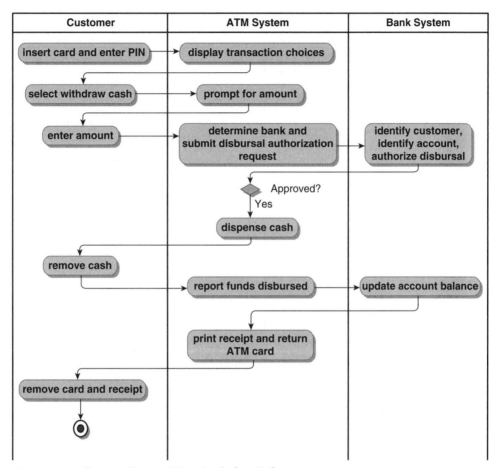

Figure 19-7: *Process-Pattern Mapping before Refinement*

A key element of this decomposition is that, from the perspective of the Customer and the Bank System, nothing has changed. Their interactions remain the same despite the decomposition of the ATM System. This is the core requirement of mapping refinement.

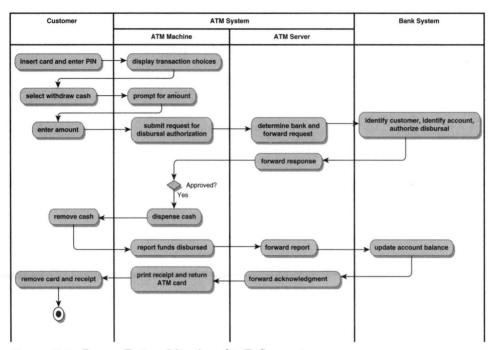

Figure 19-8: *Process-Pattern Mapping after Refinement*

Reference Architecture as the Entire Solution

There are two possible approaches for leveraging reference architectures in defining solutions. One occurs when the reference architecture encompasses the entire solution. The other, considered in the following section, occurs when the reference architecture represents only a fragment of the solution.

When the reference architecture encompasses the entire solution, the solution can be developed from the reference architecture exclusively through the process of refinement. Consider the reference architecture for a query that was considered back in Chapter 4. Let's look at building a query that finds books based upon the author's name.

Process Model Refinement

Refining the query reference architecture process model into the specific book query is relatively straightforward (Figure 19-9). Most of the

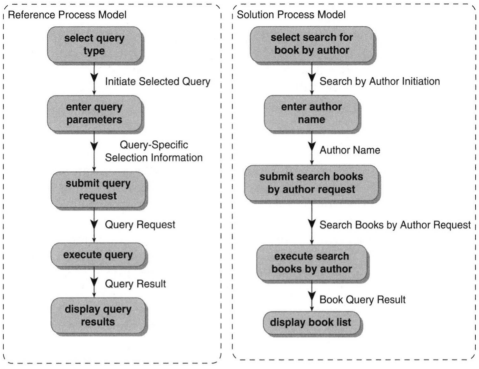

Figure 19-9: *Refining the Query Process Model*

refinement consists of making the terminology specific to the type of query.

Perhaps the most interesting aspect of the process refinement is detailing the query result. Figure 19-10 shows the refined result.

Figure 19-10: *Refining the Query Result*

Architecture Pattern Refinement

Refining the architecture pattern for the query again adds detail (see Figure 19-11). The browsers being supported are Internet Explorer version 8 and Firefox. The application server will be a WebSphere server. The service will be called the Book Search Service, and the back-end system will be an Oracle database.

Mapping Refinement

The mapping refinement for the query example is straightforward as well. The reference architecture mapping is shown in Figure 19-12 (this is actually a copy of Figure 4-4, repeated here for convenience).

The refined mapping is shown in Figure 19-13.

This particular example is notable for the lack of change in taking the reference architecture and building the solution. This is actually good news—it means that there are no significant design decisions to be made in applying the reference architecture. All the decision-making has already been done. From a project perspective, the result is lower cost and faster time to complete. From an enterprise perspective, the result is consistent implementation of a well-considered design across multiple projects. There is a worthwhile return on the up-front investment in creating the reference architecture.

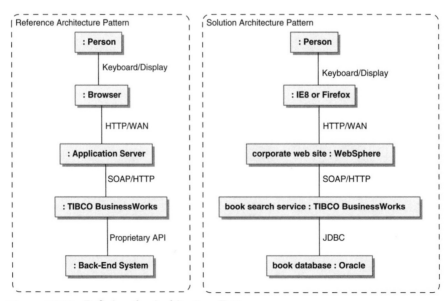

Figure 19-11: *Refining the Architecture Pattern*

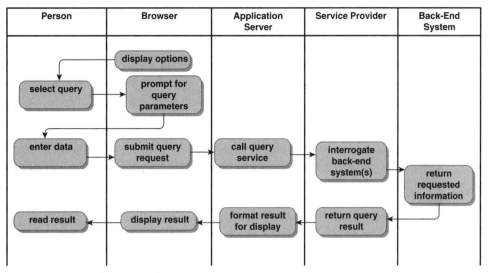

Figure 19-12: *Reference Architecture Mapping*

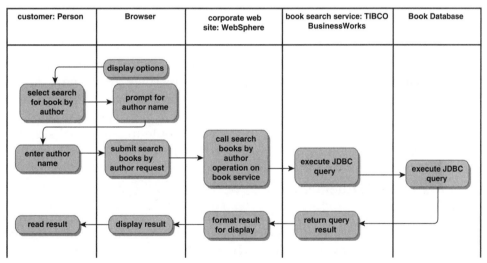

Figure 19-13: *Solution Mapping after Refinement*

Reference Architecture as a Solution Fragment

Another scenario for applying reference architectures arises when the reference architecture is used as a fragment of the solution. Let's take a look at refining the membership validation service in this manner.

Architecture Pattern Refinement

Figure 19-14 shows a possible refinement of the Membership Validation Service. The proposed refinement uses a single ActiveMatrix composite that contains two components: a Mediation Flow used for routing and a BusinessWorks process to access the local databases.

This refinement employs a number of reference architectures from earlier chapters. The Validate Membership Service Interface, provided by the mediation flow, has been promoted twice using two different transports. This is a refinement of the Straight-Wire Mapping pattern's transport mapping use case from Chapter 14. The promoted services provide appropriate policy enforcement points for access control policies (Chapter 13).

Using the mediation flow as a router is a refinement of the Routing pattern, also from Chapter 14. Using BusinessWorks to access the local database is a refinement of the ActiveMatrix-initiated Direct Interaction via non-ActiveMatrix-supported protocols using BusinessWorks initiating the interaction (Chapter 15). The direct access of the partner system is an instance of the Direct Interaction via ActiveMatrix-Supported Protocols from the same chapter.

Inserting the refined structure of the service into the initial architecture pattern yields the refined architecture pattern of Figure 19-15. This is a strict refinement of the original pattern: There are no new design elements or communications channels. Note that this architecture can be readily extended to accommodate other back-end systems: The mediation flow can be easily modified to route to additional systems either by direct interaction or using adapters.

Mapping Refinement

The mapping provided in the original architecture was generic with respect to the back-end systems. With the refinement of the service structure, it is now necessary to be specific about the mapping details in each of the cases. Figure 19-16 shows the mapping when the back-end system is the local database. Here the database access component (BusinessWorks) has an interface that is identical to the overall service, and the transformation of the request into a database query takes place within this component.

Figure 19-17 shows the mapping when the back-end system is the partner system. It has a SOAP over HTTP interface of its own, and the transformation and invocation activities are carried out by the Mediation component.

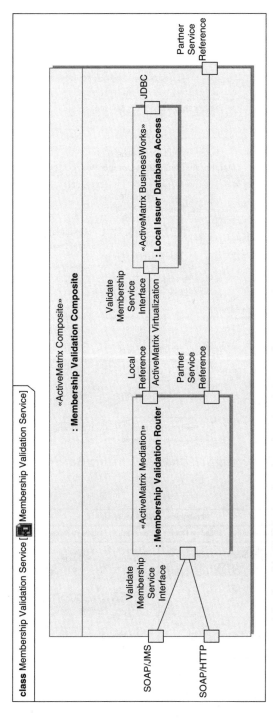

Figure 19-14: *Membership Validation Service after Applying Reference Architectures*

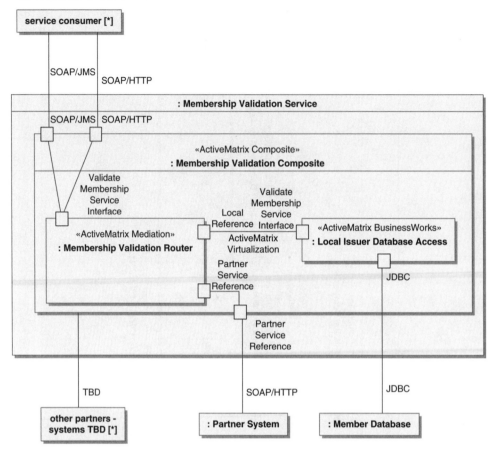

Figure 19-15: *Refined Membership Validation Architecture Pattern*

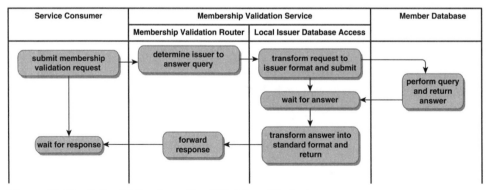

Figure 19-16: *Refined Mapping—Local Database Variant*

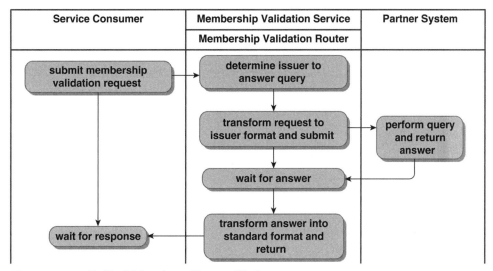

Figure 19-17: *Refined Mapping—Partner Variant*

Summary

A solution architecture defines the structure and organization of a solution. It presents the same three views as any architecture: process models, architecture pattern, and process-pattern mappings.

A lot of detail has to be added to the solution architecture to get the complete solution. To maintain the validity of the reasoning that went into defining the architecture, implementation has to be conducted through a process of refinement. Refinement adds detail without altering structure. This is accomplished by adding sub-structure to activities in the process model and participants in the architecture pattern. These refinements require refinement of the mappings as well.

Reference architectures can be employed in the creation of solutions in two ways. When the reference architecture encompasses the entire scope of the solution, the solution can be constructed from the reference architecture entirely through the process of refinement. When the reference architecture encompasses only a fragment of the solution, refinement of the reference architecture yields a fragment of the solution.

Most of the reference architectures presented in this book are intended to be used as fragments of a solution. The Membership Validation Service example in this chapter contains a number of examples of this type of reference architecture utilization.

Chapter 20

Beyond Fundamentals

Although this book covers a lot of material, it barely scratches the surface when it comes to building solutions. The primary focus of the book has been on understanding architecture and the architectural building blocks that are available for solutions.

Recap

The exploration began by examining how the focus of design for projects has evolved from system-centric to process-centric. The scope of designs is larger as well, including both people and systems: the total architecture. Three important architecture views were explored: process models, architecture patterns, and process-pattern mappings. Reference architectures were explored as abstracted architectures, providing generic solutions to generic problems.

The need for architecture as an essential activity in the development process was identified. Information was presented showing that the architecture activity can reduce project duration by up to 25%. The roles of both project and enterprise architect were explored, emphasizing the importance of the enterprise role in guiding multiple projects to converge on a single coherent architecture.

An overview of the major TIBCO products typically employed in a distributed solution was presented. The architectural highlights of TIBCO Enterprise Message Service, the TIBCO ActiveMatrix product suite, and TIBCO BusinessEvents were presented along with the typical life cycles of solutions built upon these products. Included was an overview of the SCA notation that is used as the design interface in TIBCO ActiveMatrix Service Bus.

A series of design patterns were explored covering a variety of topics: two-party interactions, policies, mediation, system access, two-party coordination, and multi-party coordination. A brief overview of services was presented.

The exploration concluded with an examination of how this information can be applied to the building of solutions. The notion of refinement was introduced as a process for adding detail to an architecture without fundamentally altering it. Two different approaches for applying reference architectures to building solutions were outlined and illustrated with several examples.

Looking Ahead

The material in this book provides a foundation common to solutions built upon TIBCO products. The focus has been primarily on combining small numbers of components to solve common problems associated with making components interact, accessing systems, and coordinating their activities. Looking at real-world solutions, these are mere building blocks. There is much more to be explored.

Toward that end, this book is just the first in a series of books designed to explore more comprehensive solutions. Planned books in this Addison-Wesley series include:

- *Architecting Composite Applications and Services with TIBCO*
- *Architecting BPM Solutions with TIBCO*
- *Architecting Complex Event Processing Solutions with TIBCO*

Keep an eye out for them!

Index

A

Abstraction. *See* Reference architecture

Access control
Aspect-Oriented Design considerations, 141–143
direct interaction via ActiveMatrix-supported protocols and, 178
policy enforcement points in, 78–79, 148
standardizing using services, 212
straight-wire mapping mediation pattern and, 164

Accidental architecture, 7

ActiveMatrix adapters, 178–179

ActiveMatrix composite implementation type, 76

ActiveMatrix hosts
administration organization of, 84–86
architecture pattern and, 88–89
configuration folder, 87
creating with TIBCO Configuration Tool, 86–87
folders for, 87
overview of, 80
physical environment, 83–84
SOAP over ActiveMatrix Virtualization used only with, 178
solution life cycle and, 88–91

ActiveMatrix nodes
deploying SCA designs on, 91–96
enforcing policies in, 148, 159
example of, 78–79
within internal structure, 74–75
in logical environments, 83–84
overview of, 78
in physical environments, 83–84
as Service Bus element, 80

ActiveMatrix policy framework
accessing external systems, 150–153

accessing LDAP, 153–157
approach to, 143–144
Aspect-Oriented Design, 141–143
associating policy sets with design elements, 148–150
policy applicability, 148
policy enforcement points, 148
policy intents, 157–158
policy set templates, 146–148
policy sets, 144–146
summary review, 158–159

ActiveMatrix Virtualization transport, 123

Activities
ATM withdraw cash process example, 21–22
implementing in parallel, 23–24
process-pattern mapping, 18–19
structuring through process models, 13–16

Adapter binding type, 77

Adapter SDK, TIBCO®, 180–181

Adapters. *See* TIBCO ActiveMatrix adapters

Add Resource dialog, policy in LDAP, 155–156

Administration
stand-alone EMS tool for, 69
using Administrator. *See* TIBCO ActiveMatrix® Administrator

Advice, in Aspect-Oriented Design, 142

Agile development process, 37

AMX hosts. *See* ActiveMatrix hosts

Announcements
bridge delivery semantics for, 137–138
Out-Only message pattern, 120–121
requests vs., 133
topic delivery semantics for, 137

The Power of Now®

TIBCO Education

You've read the book... now take action!

TIBCO Education is offering companion courses for each of the books in the architecture series from TIBCO Press. Each course will be released to coincide with the publication of its companion book. The planned series includes:

- ARC 701: TIBCO Architecture Fundamentals (available now)
- ARC 702: Architecting Composite Applications and Services with TIBCO
- ARC 703: Architecting BPM Solutions with TIBCO
- ARC 704: Architecting Complex Event Processing Solutions with TIBCO

Use these and other TIBCO courses to experience, first hand, the unprecedented creative and innovative capabilities of TIBCO technologies. TIBCO Education provides the training courses, study materials, practical methods, and technology that you need to accelerate your success.

The rest is up to you...

To find a convenient TIBCO Training Center near you, or to learn more about training available to a wide range of professionals, visit the TIBCO Education website at http://www.tibco.com/services/educational